The World of Copley

Other Publications:

TIME-LIFE LIBRARY OF ART

The World of Copley
1738-1815

by Alfred Frankenstein
and
the Editors of TIME-LIFE BOOKS

TIME-LIFE BOOKS, ALEXANDRIA, VIRGINIA

Time-Life Books Inc.
is a wholly owned subsidiary of
TIME INCORPORATED

FOUNDER: Henry R. Luce 1898-1967
Editor-in-Chief: Hedley Donovan
Chairman of the Board: Andrew Heiskell
President: James R. Shepley
Vice Chairman: Roy E. Larsen
Corporate Editor: Ralph Graves

TIME-LIFE BOOKS INC.
MANAGING EDITOR: Jerry Korn
Executive Editor: David Maness
Assistant Managing Editors: Dale Brown, Martin Mann
Art Director: Tom Suzuki
Chief of Research: David L. Harrison
Director of Photography: Melvin L. Scott
Senior Text Editors: William Frankel, Diana Hirsh
Assistant Art Director: Arnold C. Holeywell

CHAIRMAN: Joan D. Manley
President: John D. McSweeney
Executive Vice Presidents: Carl G. Jaeger, David J. Walsh
Vice President and Secretary: Paul R. Stewart
Treasurer and General Manager: John Steven Maxwell
Business Manager: Peter B. Barnes
Mail Order Sales Director: John L. Canova
Public Relations Director: Nicholas Benton
Personnel Director: Beatrice T. Dobie

TIME-LIFE LIBRARY OF ART
SERIES EDITOR: Robert Morton
Editorial Staff for *The World of Copley:*
Text Editor: L. Robert Tschirky
Designer: Paul Jensen
Staff Writers: John von Hartz, Suzanne Seixas,
Carolyn Tasker
Chief Researcher: Martha T. Goolrick
Researchers: Adrian Condon, Jill N. Beasley,
Evelyn Constable, Catherine Ireys, Susan Jonas,
Susanna Seymour
Assistant to the Designer: Mervyn Clay

EDITORIAL PRODUCTION
Production Editor: Douglas B. Graham
Operations Manager: Gennaro C. Esposito
Assistant Production Editor: Feliciano Madrid
Quality Director: Robert L. Young
Assistant Quality Director: James J. Cox
Associate: Serafino J. Cambareri
Copy Staff: Susan B. Galloway (chief), Patricia Miller,
Florence Keith, Celia Beattie
Picture Department: Dolores A. Littles,
Elizabeth A. Dagenhardt
Traffic: Barbara Buzan

About the Author

A graduate of the University of Chicago, Alfred Frankenstein has been a critic and writer on the fine arts for the *San Francisco Chronicle* for more than 35 years. Mr. Frankenstein regularly contributes articles on art and music to leading periodicals. He has taught American art at New York University, Harvard and the University of California and is the author of *After the Hunt,* a study of William Harnett and other 19th Century American still-life painters.

The Consulting Editor

H. W. Janson is Professor of Fine Arts at New York University, where he is also Chairman of the Department of Fine Arts at Washington Square College. Among his many publications are *History of Art* and *The Sculpture of Donatello.*

The Consultant for This Book

Philip C. Beam is the Chairman of the Department of Art and Professor of Archaeology at Bowdoin College. For 25 years Dr. Beam was Director of the Bowdoin College Museum of Art where he is currently Curator of the Winslow Homer Collection. Among his books are *The Language of Art* and *Winslow Homer at Prout's Neck.*

On the Slipcase

This detail from Copley's *Boy with a Squirrel* reveals the artist's half brother, Henry Pelham, casually posed at a table with a pet flying squirrel. The complete painting is shown on page 58.

End Papers

These drawings, made in black and white chalk on gray-blue paper, were done by Copley as preparatory sketches for his vivid battle scene *The Death of Major Peirson,* seen in color on pages 154-155. *Front:* Copley used his own family, including his adolescent son, John Jr., as models for the frightened citizenry. *Back:* Ruling off his sketch for ease in transferring it to the larger canvas, Copley also jotted down specific notes on the colors of uniforms and accessories.

Correspondents Elisabeth Kraemer (Bonn); Margot Hapgood, Dorothy Bacon, Rosemary Young (London); Susan Jonas, Lucy T. Voulgaris (New York); Maria Vincenza Aloisi, Josephine du Brusle (Paris); Ann Natanson (Rome).

Contents

OF THE TOWN OF BOSTON IN NEW-ENGLAND AN

I

Man of Two Worlds

There is no Titian telephone exchange in Venice, and if you should call CEZanne 64-75 in Paris you would get no answer. Boston alone among major cities has named a telephone exchange after one of its celebrated painters. To be sure, computerized communication has now reduced the old COpley 2 prefix to an anonymous 262, but that is the way of our era. Mechanization has penetrated even the sacred groves of art history, and in connection with the same artist. Professor Jules David Prown of Yale, Copley's most recent biographer, used the computer to obtain statistics on the professions, incomes, politics, marital status and religious affiliations of 240 of the more than 350 men and women whose portraits Copley painted during his years in his native city.

One does not allude to the Copley telephone exchange out of mere journalistic whimsy. For many years COpley 2 meant something special to Bostonians, and the public square in Boston that still bears the artist's name maintains the meaning: in the family-proud hub of New England the possession of an ancestral portrait by Copley is a patent of aristocracy. But these cherished heirlooms also have a significance that transcends Boston and its first families.

John Singleton Copley was the foremost American artist of the 18th Century. The likenesses he painted in Boston between 1753, when he began his career, and 1774, when he left for permanent self-exile in London, were the best that colonial America had yet produced. The highly personal style he created from provincial New England roots not only profoundly influenced all American portraiture in his time but ultimately won him an honored place among the leading artists of Europe. Copley is the first American painter on record to take up his residence abroad at the instigation of European colleagues. The first picture he sent from Boston to London for exhibition, in 1766, astonished the critics; they expected no such virtuosity from a provincial artist. Even Joshua Reynolds, then dean of British painters, pronounced the work outstanding. He felt that Copley was too good for the colonies and urged him to come to the mother country and study old masters on the Continent. So did Benjamin West, an expatriate American artist who had earned acclaim in London

Boston's Long Wharf, where Copley spent his childhood, is shown here in an engraving by Paul Revere. The wharf, an extension of one of the city's main streets, was lined with warehouses, shipping-company offices and shops, including a tobacco shop run by Copley's parents. The engraving records the landing in 1768 of more than a thousand British troops—one of the measures that ultimately sparked the American Revolution.

Paul Revere: *A View of Part of the Town of Boston in New England and British Ships of War Landing Their Troops, 1768*, detail

7

and who could not foresee the day when he and Copley would be rivals. In time Copley heeded their advice.

Thus his long career falls into two distinct periods. His first 37 years saw his rise from humble beginnings on Boston's waterfront to prominence as the city's foremost portraitist. They also witnessed his one brief appearance on the stage of political history when, on the eve of the American Revolution, he singlehandedly tried to ease the tension between Whigs and Tories that was to erupt into the Boston Tea Party. His last 40 years in London, after his eyes had been opened to Europe's great works of art and traditions, brought him new triumphs in new fields of painting and, until his creative prowess declined with advancing age, he enjoyed world renown.

The styles that characterized Copley's art in these two periods were vastly different, and since his work has been preserved almost complete, it is possible to trace his artistic evolution in detail. From boyhood he knew what he wanted to do; the trouble was that he had not the vaguest idea of how to do it. No school existed in Boston to offer serious instruction to an aspiring artist, for many Bostonians still clung to old Puritan ideas that held most forms of painting to be either blasphemous or frivolous. While portraits were sanctioned because they were the only way of perpetuating the features of important citizens, most of the likenesses that young Copley may have seen were stiff, flatly colored and often crudely drawn, with small teaching value. Thus Copley had to absorb his chosen craft from elsewhere—from his engraver stepfather, from the few really talented artists in the neighborhood, and from engravings after Reynolds and other European painters. At the end of a decade of self-instruction possibly without parallel among artists for its intensity and single-mindedness, it was evident that Copley had mastered his craft, and the style he had developed clearly set his work above that of his colonial predecessors and his contemporaries as well.

Among the hallmarks of that style is a fully rounded modeling of the human figure that gives it an almost three-dimensional effect; precise contours; strong contrasts of light and shade; occasional sharp dissonances of color; and a smooth finish, with all signs of brushwork neatly concealed. Characteristic, too, is Copley's attention to textiles; he had a still-life painter's eye for them and for the vast variety of shiny, filmy, coarse and fine effects they provide. His feeling for still life also flows over into the accessories with which he often enlivened his American portraits. In his likeness of Mrs. Ezekiel Goldthwait *(pages 80-81)*, for example, the plump little lady and the bowl of fruit on the table before her are painted with exactly the same degree of interest.

Mrs. Goldthwait, with her bowl of fruit, seems a real person, and Copley's Boston world is crowded with such convincing characters. Mrs. Samuel Waldo appears so modest that one wonders how she ever got married, Mrs. Richard Skinner is the Yankee aristocrat to the life, Nathaniel Sparhawk *(page 82)* exudes pomposity, and one would do well to bring along a lawyer in making a business deal with Mrs. Humphrey Devereux. Copley had no predilections when it came to sitters. He not only ran through the entire range of human personality, male and female,

The early New England Puritans produced a great deal of folk art. This scene of Adam and Eve in the Garden of Eden was embroidered of crewels (twisted threads) on linen in 1760 by Mary Sarah Titcomb. Picturemaking of this kind was common in homes. Girls were expected to learn needlework, and their creations served not only as decorative hangings but also a more practical purpose: the fabric helped block the drafts that whistled through wooden walls.

young and old, but he showed no partiality when it came to painting members of the political factions that divided pre-Revolutionary Boston. Just when it seems that the artist was especially sympathetic in depicting Revolutionary red-hots like Paul Revere *(page 84)*, his portraits of Tories like Isaac Winslow and his wife all but step from their frames and take your hand.

The living presence of Copley's Boston portraits marks him as the first American painter to reassure one that there are no period people, only period costumes, and a gallery full of Copleys provides a survey of the human comedy akin to what might be seen today on Boston Common or any other place the world reserves for people-watching. The self-satisfaction of matronly Mrs. Isaac Smith, in her brocaded chair, is as ageless as the warmth and intensity of young Mrs. Nathaniel Allen under her wide hat or the slightly devilish expression of the Reverend Thomas Cary as he looks up from reading his Bible. Timeless, too, is the elderly dignity of Mrs. Thomas Boylston *(page 77)*, with her keen but patient face and her frail old lady's body scarcely concealed by her brown silk dress and black lace shawl. In her portrait Copley powerfully suggests the winning through from pioneer plainness to prosperity that is the essence of the American success story.

However, after full tribute is paid to Copley's realism, his perception of character, the beauty of his textiles and the charm of his accessories, the fact remains that in his Boston years he exploited a very limited repertoire of poses and dramatic devices and that his draftsmanship sometimes fell short of his intentions. Time and again he seated people before polished mahogany tables, with their hands or bodies reflected in the mirrorlike surfaces. No colonial artist before him had attempted anything so tricky, but because he so often repeated it this effective device takes on the look of a mannerism. On the other hand he may have intended it as a salute from a craftsman in one field to notable craftsmen in another: there were great cabinetmakers in Copley's Boston, and it is no accident that their works and his are displayed today in the same gallery in Boston's Museum of Fine Arts. Equally as repetitious as his reflecting tables was Copley's habit of showing the prominent men of his time in informal attire, relaxed in rich dressing gowns and wearing velvet house caps to conceal heads shaved to accommodate a wig in public. And not infrequently—even in his most mature productions before he left for Europe —he portrayed them with poorly proportioned heads, arms or torsos. He also developed a curious way of showing them apparently in the act of kicking themselves out of their own portraits; over and over again a gray-stockinged leg comes down and its foot is awkwardly buried in a corner of the frame.

On crossing the Atlantic in 1774 Copley entered a new universe. At last he could satisfy a long craving to study at first hand the masterworks of European art he had known only through hearsay or engravings. Almost at once changes began to appear in his style. After a six-week visit to London, he spent 14 rapturous months in the cities and galleries of Italy, and in a letter to a friend spoke of the "luxury in seeing" that the Continent afforded him. Hence in the first portrait he painted abroad

—that of Mr. and Mrs. Ralph Izard of South Carolina, then living in Rome—there is an unaccustomed clutter of accessories: a marble-topped Italian Renaissance table, classical statuary, an ancient Greek vase and a glimpse of the Colosseum in the distance. Because these things symbolized the new world of visual experience now opening up to him, it is no wonder Copley used them all in the Izard double likeness; and thereafter he sometimes tended to crowd a little too much into his portraits.

His "luxury in seeing" also made itself felt in the broadening of his subject matter. Far removed from portraiture was the Ascension of Christ that he painted in Italy after studying the techniques of Raphael and other old masters. Its many figures grouped before a landscape made it a much more complex composition than anything Copley had attempted in America, and he handled it remarkably well. But most remarkable of all was the fact that the artist from Puritan Boston had come so soon to paint so popish a picture. Any proper Bostonian of his time would have been shocked at the mere notion.

When Copley returned to settle in London, his style and range of subject matter changed even more markedly under British influence. It is futile to evaluate the work of his London period as compared with his work in Boston, but it is instructive to see the difference—a difference so dramatic as to suggest that the cultural gap between Americans and Englishmen was much greater before America cut loose from England than it has been ever since.

For one thing, England enjoyed a gallantry, courtliness and extravagance of dress beside which Copley's provincial world seemed provincial indeed. These qualities were reflected in his London portraits. While many were as simple and realistic as any he did in America, others were painted to suit the prevailing British taste for more elegant, idealized likenesses set against imaginative, accessory-filled backgrounds. In Copley's English paintings, color takes on new significance: he no longer concealed his brushwork, but exploited it in dabs, streaks and dashes of paint; light no longer models forms as palpably as in the Boston days, but is impressionistically broken up.

Furthermore, Copley's British audience had a much broader religious outlook and encouraged him to paint other Biblical subjects that, like Christ's Ascension, would have been taboo in Boston. In addition London was conscious of its status as a European capital and a crossroad of cultural currents that scarcely touched New England. Among these currents in the last quarter of the 18th Century was a continuing interest in classical learning. Thus Copley found himself surrounded by painters of scenes from classical mythology and he briefly joined their ranks. Englishmen, too, were proud of their long history, and Copley catered to that pride in a series of historical pictures. It was his painting of these that led to his rivalry with Benjamin West. The Pennsylvania-born West had built no small part of his reputation on large pictures of heroic deaths in recent British history—those of General James Wolfe at Quebec and Lord Nelson at Trafalgar, for example—and so Copley painted even larger canvases of such heroic deaths as that of young Major Francis Peirson as he defended the island of Jersey against French invaders.

Moreover, even before he painted such newly accepted subjects as stirring events from past and recent British history, Copley experimented with a dramatic scene of everyday life—an innovation that presaged the Romantic art of the 19th Century. In art, centuries do not begin precisely at midnight on the first day of their earliest year. In this sense the 19th Century was at least a decade a-borning, and Copley was one of those who assisted at its birth.

If there is a hollow ring today to the historical paintings produced by Copley and his contemporaries, with their glorification of war, nationalism, and military and political leaders, the major work by Copley that foreshadows the Romantic school has values as powerful in our time as when the painting was new. Now called *Watson and the Shark (page 148)*, it shows a nude youth struggling in the waters of Havana's harbor before the onslaught of a huge, chimerical fish, while a group of men in the boat strains to save him and a figure in the prow prepares to harpoon the shark with a boat hook. All this adds up to one of the most striking early statements of Romanticism's essentially pessimistic view of the world. The original title of the picture was simply *A Young Man and a Shark*. Copley's intention, in other words, had been not merely to record one individual's swimming accident but to extract a generalized statement from a perilous encounter with the forces of evil. The repercussions of that prophetic work were to be felt in art, European as well as American, for a long time to come.

Mark Rothko, the contemporary American artist, has observed that "the great figure painters have this in common: their portraits resemble each other far more than they recall the peculiarities of a particular model. In a sense they have painted one character in all their work. What is indicated here is that the artist's real model is an ideal which embraces all of human drama rather than the appearance of a particular individual." One might amend this in Copley's case to suggest that the two worlds in which he lived—up-and-coming Boston and cosmopolitan London—presented him with two successive ideal models. More than any other artist of his period, he effectively spanned those worlds.

Copley was psychologically prepared to make the long leap across the Atlantic well before he actually did so. As early as November 1766 —almost a decade before he left Boston—he wrote to his fellow American Benjamin West in London: "In this Country . . . there is no example of Art, except what is to be met with in a few prints indifferently executed, from which it is not possible to learn much." Such complaints about America's poverty in works of art, and about the lack of sophistication of his provincial patrons, are a constant litany in Copley's correspondence with friends and colleagues abroad. "A taste of painting is too much Wanting to afford any kind of helps," he declared a few weeks later in another letter to West, "and was it not for preserving the resemblance of particular persons, painting would not be known in the plac[e]. The people generally regard it no more than any other usefull trade, as they sometimes term it, like that of a Carpenter, tailor or shew maker, not as one of the most noble Arts in the World. Which is not a little Mortifying to me." On yet another occasion he complained to West that nature had been

Early New England churches permitted no art inside, but their adjacent graveyards were filled with headstones that were often remarkably decorative. The Reverend Jonathan Pierpont's tombstone *(above)* bore verses extolling his rectitude and, on side panels *(detail below)*, a bas-relief portrait of the Massachusetts clergyman clutching a Bible. His cherubic face is a symbol of his piety rather than a facsimile of his features.

The austerity of Old Ship Meetinghouse at Hingham, Massachusetts, reflects the Puritan belief that nothing should distract a worshiper's attention from his God. Thus no stained glass, no pictures, no sculptures were allowed. Like other early New England meetinghouses, Old Ship was used both for prayer and for town assemblies. Named for its beamed ceiling, which resembles the interior of a ship's hull, the building was erected in 1681 and is the only surviving example of its type.

his only instructor, and asserted that Boston had not contained a single portrait "worthy to be call'd a Picture within my memory."

In fact, the situation was by no means as barren as Copley implied. Part of his discontent stemmed from the praise that had greeted his first picture to be exhibited in London, *Boy with a Squirrel (page 58)*. Such plaudits whetted his appetite for distant places where Art was Art. But while the capital of the Massachusetts Bay Colony was not, to be sure, London or Paris, it had a far broader and more well-developed tradition of art than Copley's comments would indicate, and he had himself been fundamentally conditioned by it. Like so many Americans then and later, he took his own tradition so much for granted that he did not even recognize it as a tradition.

Art in colonial New England—like everything else in that part of the world—had been deeply if unconsciously affected by religious taboos. The Pilgrims, whose break with the Church of England led them to found the first settlement in Massachusetts in 1620, might disagree with the even sterner-minded Puritans who followed them about many aspects of doctrine, but on one point they were in complete harmony: they brooked no fancywork in the House of God. Their churches were plain and spare, and, in the scheme of things, to paint religious subjects was inconceivable. Furthermore, most people in the Massachusetts Bay Colony were not learned folk; paintings of literary, mythological or historical subjects meant nothing to them, and may well have appeared, at least to some of them, as sinful. Finally, both Pilgrims and Puritans viewed the next world as preferable to this one, and no one among them was inspired to paint the local scenery of what was often to them an extremely harsh land. No religious theme, no historic or literary anecdote, no landscape—there was only one subject left for a painter: the faces and figures of the colonists themselves.

A handful of such paintings survives from 17th Century Boston, primarily dating from 1670 or thereabouts. There was good reason for this timing. The earliest settlers of the region did not even have the shelter of huts; they slept in shallow, scooped-out places in the ground protected from the wind by rough screens of reeds and leaves. Under such circumstances, no one paints portraits. Half a century went by before life became sufficiently stable—homes and churches built, roads laid out, towns organized—to permit such luxuries as portraits.

The first towns of New England were named after towns of Old England from which the settlers came—Boston, Hull, Plymouth and so on. In addition to place names, the settlers brought with them the architecture, costumes and habits of life they had known at home. So far as portraits were concerned, they knew nothing about the courtly likenesses fashionable in London, and if they had known about them they would have scorned them. But hanging in the guildhalls and other public buildings of the smaller English towns, and in some of the outlying manor houses, were older and half-forgotten portraits, painted in a more restrained style that had flourished all over England in the 16th Century but had been pushed aside in the 17th. In these paintings the subject's head was bathed in a full, unwavering light and shown in great detail. The body, however, received little or no light and was scarcely delineated at all; it appeared as a mere silhouette from which the hands suddenly emerged to be treated with as much attention to detail as the head. Often the hands grasped a book or some other accessory. This highly schematized style is what the emigrants to New England knew. It was at least a century and a half out of date by 1670, but the New Englanders could not have cared less. And this was the style that they preferred for the first portraits painted on American soil.

Collectively the painters of these portraits were known as limners, because the flatness and patternlike composition of nearly all their works recalled the limning, or illumination, in medieval manuscripts. Probably they were not artists at all in the ordinary sense of the word. Hardheaded practicality was the keynote in early New England; as one colonist put it, "The Plow-Man that raiseth Grain is more serviceable to Mankind than the Painter who draws only to please the Eye." Thus many limners earned their main livelihood in utilitarian trades that had nothing to do with art—farming, shopkeeping, woodworking, shipbuilding. Others were professional house painters, sign painters or silversmiths who made art a side line. They would paint anything from decorations on a fire bucket to memorial portraits of the dead and likenesses of the living. A full century was to elapse before anyone engaged in this pursuit would take on such airs as to claim membership among the practitioners of "one of the most noble Arts in the World," as Copley called it.

With one or two exceptions, the names of the earliest colonial painters have been lost. The works they produced represent a rough-and-ready frontier adaptation of the English 16th Century manner, often created not with specialized artists' materials but with house or ship's

So similar in style that they might almost have been painted by the same artist, these two portraits were produced about 75 years apart and on different continents. The Tudor portrait of the Earl of Salisbury *(above)* was painted in England in 1602. The likeness of John Freake *(top)* was painted in America about 1674. Colonial portraiture was much in debt to the Tudor style, which went out of fashion in London, but remained popular and influential in the provinces.

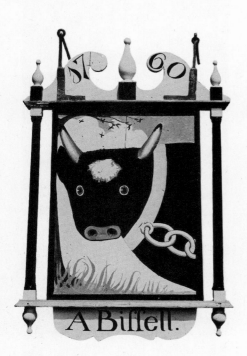

Typical of the primitively painted, brightly colored signboards that hung in front of shops and taverns in colonial towns is the one above. It advertises an inn at South Windsor, Connecticut, operated by A. Bissell, and probably called the Bull's Head. Many artists of 18th Century America began their careers traveling about the countryside painting such signs on wooden shingles, since this was one of the few practical outlets available for creative talent.

paint and brushes of crudely fashioned broom straw. Their personalities, however, are clearly stamped on their work, and their individual approaches can be clearly distinguished.

The Davenport Limner—so called because his touch was first identified in portraits of the family of the Reverend Doctor John Davenport—remained most consistently within the framework of the 16th Century style. In every work by his hand discovered thus far, he limited himself to portraits of ministers and civic leaders, the respected elders of the community. The Freake Limner devoted himself entirely to family portraits. His best-known paintings are of the dignified Gibbs children and of young Mrs. Freake and her infant *(page 100)*—the work that has lent him his current name. A third limner whose name is known—Captain Thomas Smith—painted the rugged middle-aged men-at-arms whom a frontier community desperately needed for its protection. Smith was a seafarer. His voyages may have taken him to Europe, and there, perhaps, he saw some portraits by Dutch or English masters; in any event he alone, among early limners, succeeded in making his figures look like more than paper cutouts: he softened their outlines with an envelope of air so that they seem to stand forth from their background.

Despite the variety in the sort of people they portrayed, these and other limners had one thing in common in their approach to their sitters. Surprisingly, they portrayed New Englanders of the second half of the 17th Century in the fanciest of fancy dress, with ribbons and fine laces, jewels, gloves and rich fabrics. No doubt these people posed for their pictures in their Sunday best; but the point is that they were not dressed in the ascetic garments in which tradition so often claims they were clothed. There was a good deal more gaiety and worldliness in Puritan life than most history books admit, and the costumes in these portraits are prime evidence of that fact.

The 1670 style continued into the first quarter of the 18th Century. One of its last major expressions is the shrewd, unforgettable face of Anne Pollard *(page 101)*, painted, according to the unknown artist's inscription on the canvas, in 1721, when Mistress Pollard was 100 years old. She claimed to have been the first person off the boat when Boston was settled in 1630 by colonists from Charlestown across the Charles River, and she is reputed to have run a tavern in Boston in her last years. The existence of taverns is itself indicative of the fact that by the early 18th Century Boston had become less a theocracy and much more a commercial center. It was no longer a stronghold of Puritan dissent but the hub of a thriving royal province. Abuses in the governing of the Massachusetts Bay Colony had resulted in revocation of its colonial charter by the Crown in 1684, and now Boston was headquarters for governors sent from England. Their more sophisticated rule, combined with a flourishing trade, was bringing about a wider tolerance of worldly ways.

In 1729, just eight years after the painting of Anne Pollard's portrait and nine years before Copley's birth, the whole picture of art in New England began to change profoundly. The immediate cause was the arrival from abroad of the first fully trained professional artist to take up his residence in America.

John Smibert, a Scotsman then 40 years old, had crossed the Atlantic from England in a party headed by Dean George Berkeley. This idealistic Irish churchman had become convinced that the future of European civilization would be worked out on American soil; he had even set forth his idea in a poem containing the now-famous line, "Westward the course of empire takes its way."

The course of empire, as Berkeley saw it, needed minds to guide it, and so he conceived a plan to establish a university in the New World. Believing that favorable climate had played a great part in making Athens the intellectual capital of antiquity, he decided to locate the university in that part of the Western Hemisphere whose weather was most nearly Athenian. This, voyagers told him, was Bermuda.

Berkeley and the faculty members for his projected school—Smibert was to teach painting, drawing and architecture—never reached Bermuda. The Dean had injudiciously left England without the funds the British government had pledged him for setting up the university. After a stopover of more than two years in Newport in the Rhode Island colony—a more settled and civilized place than Bermuda—where he waited in vain for a ship bringing the money, Berkeley returned, disenchanted, to England. That was the end of the Bermuda project, unless the naming of the site of the University of California, 120 years later, may be regarded as its fulfillment. Smibert stayed behind to hazard his fortunes in the rising little metropolis of Boston. The noted writer and enthusiastic patron of the arts Horace Walpole, whom he had known in London, shed some light on this decision. Apparently Smibert had joined with the visionary Berkeley not as an adventurer seeking new worlds, but simply as a craftsman who, in Walpole's words, "was enchanted with a plan that he thought promised him tranquility and an honest subsistence in a healthful Elysian climate."

Smibert had studied painting and possibly also architecture in Rome and London, and had achieved a modest reputation among British portrait painters, but obviously had shown no promise of pre-eminence among them. Thus he had little to lose by settling in Boston, and as the first full-fledged painter in colonial America he had much to gain. A year after his arrival, when he held a public showing of his work—America's first recorded art exhibition—it was greeted with eulogistic poems in the newspapers. Never before had Boston seen anything so expert, so stylish and so penetrating in characterization. Smibert remained in Boston's high esteem until his death in 1751. He also dabbled in architecture, designing the city's original Faneuil Hall, which was erected in 1742 as a market and hall for town meetings. The building was enlarged to its present size in 1805.

Boston's famous landmark, Faneuil Hall, seen in this 1789 engraving, was originally designed by the English-born artist John Smibert to serve as a combination market and meetinghouse. Completed in 1742 but gutted by fire 19 years later, the hall was rebuilt according to Smibert's design. When the city's growth dictated an expansion of the building in 1805, the new architect painstakingly retained many features of the original structure but doubled its width and added a third floor.

Among the paintings that contributed to Smibert's enthusiastic reception in Boston was a portrait of Dean Berkeley and his entourage, known as *The Bermuda Group (pages 26-27).* It was completed in November of 1729 while Berkeley was still in Newport, and it hung in Smibert's studio for the rest of his life. One could make a case for this painting as the most influential single canvas in American art history; certainly it was the most influential of colonial times. All of Boston's aspiring artists haunted Smibert's rooms. Partly this was because Smibert imported and sold artists' materials as well as engravings after English portraits, partly because he had brought from Europe oil copies he had made of paintings by Titian, Van Dyck and other old masters that gave the young Bostonians their only inkling of what made great painters great. But the major attraction of Smibert's rooms was the Berkeley picture, the largest, most elaborately composed canvas yet seen on the North American continent (and also the largest and most complex work of Smibert's career). Boston artists, in time including Copley, were to reveal their debt to it in some of their own major efforts.

Nearly eight feet wide and more than five feet high, *The Bermuda Group* contains seven adults and a baby; until its appearance, according to all existing evidence, no New England painter had ever tried to represent even two adults in a single composition, and only rarely an adult and child. Smibert showed his eight subjects sitting and standing around a table that is covered with a rich Oriental rug. The adults are orchestrated in a variety of poses. Profile opposes profile, and a figure standing at the group's left leans slightly forward. This device carries the eye downward to the seated figures, one of whom is Berkeley's wife holding their child on her lap. Then the eye is drawn upward again to rest, ultimately, on the tallest figure in the company, the Dean himself, standing at the far right and gazing meditatively as if into the future. Berkeley's breadth and heft counterweight all the other people in the picture. Only one man is nearly as tall as he is—the figure at the extreme left. Unlike Berkeley, this man does not peer into unknowable realms; he surveys the here and now, and his bright eyes are fixed on the viewer with remarkable intensity. The man is John Smibert. His self-portrait suggests pride and assertiveness, although there is little in the record of his life to bear this out. As Horace Walpole put it, he was "a silent and modest man, who abhorred the finesse of some of his profession."

Smibert's characterizations of the members of Berkeley's party are less than brilliant, and there is a certain awkwardness in the poses of individual figures and in the composition as a whole. But its very complexity entranced its Boston viewers, and so did its use of color and texture. Boston had never seen the likes of its dove grays, rich browns, deep blues and golden yellow, and nothing even remotely approaching its realistically portrayed broadcloth, velvet, silk and linen; the Turkish rug covering the table must have seemed a miracle of simulation to artistically inexperienced colonials.

The Bermuda Group is an excellent example of what 18th Century England called a "conversation piece"—a picture showing a group of people, friends or family members, in a relaxed, informal pose. William Hogarth, the great engraver and pictorial satirist, was the first English artist to make extensive and dramatic use of this device. Since he and Smibert had been contemporaries in London, Smibert may have gotten the idea from Hogarth's works. There is another interesting parallel between the two artists: both tended to portray elderly men as bright-eyed, lively old codgers. Indeed, the aging but by no means decrepit gentlemen depicted by Smibert, such as Nathaniel Byfield, are his most memorable people.

The formula he established for such portraits was totally beyond the imagination or capacity of the 1670 limners; usually the paintings were oval-shaped and the sitter was shown bust length, with one shoulder forward and the rest of the body receding in space. Smibert's women are less successful than his men. As a rule their faces are not as strikingly individual, and repeatedly they are presented according to a standard 18th Century English pattern—seated, wearing blue with white ruching at the cleavage, and with a long curl of hair coyly coming from the back of the head to be draped over one shoulder.

Smibert produced his most individual and most influential work in the years immediately after his arrival in Boston. Over the course of his 22-year career there his style became progressively less lively, more rigid, badly articulated and closer to the work of the 17th Century limners. He was isolated, out of touch with developments in English portraiture, and he had few rivals to keep him alert.

One worthy competitor, however, was a strange, enigmatic figure named Robert Feke. Feke drifted into Boston and into history around 1740 and drifted out again a decade later. A fairly detailed description of him survives. A doctor who met him wrote: "This man has exactly the phiz of a painter, having a long, pale face, sharp nose, large eyes—with which he looked at you steadfastly—long curled black hair, a delicate white hand, and long fingers." Almost nothing else is known about Feke except that he painted portraits in Philadelphia and Newport as well as in Boston. Some scholars believe that he was born on Long Island. If so, he was the first identifiable native American to become a painter of major significance.

Many of Feke's portraits are among the most elegant and idealistic ever painted on this side of the Atlantic. They totally belie the common belief that the American tradition in art is essentially blunt, realistic and down to earth. Only his earliest known picture fits that description. A group portrait of Isaac Royall of Boston and his family (*page 27*), it is clearly a paraphrase of Smibert's *Bermuda Group*. But the people in Smibert's painting form a fluent, varied design, whereas Feke's figures—three ladies with a child seated at a table and young Mr. Royall standing stiffly at the right—are set forth primly and squarely, all five with the same expressionless stare. And where Smibert's Turkish rug serves a subordinate role as an element of decoration, Feke's Turkish rug jumps out of the canvas as it might in the work of a folk painter.

His people never lost their look of wide-eyed placidity, but within a short time Feke conquered the crudities of the Royall group and established the imaginative style of portraiture for which he is noted. Most of his paintings have dreamlike backgrounds that bear little resemblance to reality, and bodies and faces so freely painted that they tend toward abstraction. In addition, Feke's portraits of men frequently achieved a nobility new to American art through his use of a pose so characteristic that we may call it the Feke stance. When painting full-length or three-quarter-length figures, he frequently showed the sitter with hand on hip, one or two fingers extended. This hand pulled back the sitter's coat in a long, gracefully curving line to reveal the richly embroidered waistcoat beneath. Even in his portrait of Brigadier General Samuel Waldo, one of the commanders of the British expedition that seized French-held Louisbourg in Nova Scotia, Feke has his subject strutting hand on hip while below him the English batteries blast away at the town. Feke did not invent his "stance." It appeared in many fashionable English portraits of the period, but no one handled it with his force and magnificence.

Feke's women are even more noteworthy than his men. Usually they are seated, and they display tightly laced waists, large breasts that seem about to burst from low-cut dresses: their upper bodies appear to be set upon immense bases produced by the billowing of silks over ample thighs. Again the prototype of the pose can be found in British portraiture, but Feke gave it a solemnity and grandeur entirely his own.

How he became aware of the English practice is unrecorded. Perhaps he saw engravings like those Smibert imported; perhaps he had some contact with the originals. He may have traveled to England; no one knows enough about the facts of his life to rule out that possibility. In any event engravings of English portraits were liberally imitated, paraphrased and plagiarized by American colonial painters, Copley included, for a long while to come.

Another portrait painter active in Boston around Feke's time was John Greenwood, a friend of Copley's stepfather. He was destined to make his single but historic contribution to the American tradition far from New England. Greenwood was born into a wealthy Boston home in 1727. Despite early financial reverses that caused him to be apprenticed for a while to an engraver and sign painter, he did not take life too seriously. There was a strong vein of caricature in Greenwood's Boston portraits. And, while he employed many of the same conventions of pose and stance as Feke, he used them in a rough-and-tumble way, without a trace of Feke's thoughtful elegance.

Greenwood left Boston for good in 1752. He went first to Surinam (Dutch Guiana), a stopping place for Yankee merchant ships; later he turned up in London and forsook painting to become an art dealer. While in South America he reportedly painted more than a hundred portraits, but if any survive, their whereabouts is a mystery. But around 1820 one Greenwood canvas—and an astonishing one—found its way out of Surinam to North America.

The picture is *Sea Captains Carousing in Surinam,* the first known instance of genre painting to be produced by a native American. It is crude in its draftsmanship, hectic in its lighting and violently drunk in its rhythms, all of which is appropriate to the subject: a group of righteous, psalm-singing New England sea captains in a tavern, swilling punch by the bowlful, dancing, playing cards, puking and generally carrying on like New England mariners who are safely out of New England. In this work, produced in 1757, Greenwood launched the American practice of painting everyday scenes in an atmosphere of satire and exposure of social evils. The spirit of the work is far different from the sweetness and light that characterized genre scenes in America in the next century.

Young John Singleton Copley could not, of course, have seen *Sea Captains,* but he undoubtedly did know Greenwood's earlier Boston portraits.

They are reflected in some of his own first awkward attempts at portraiture. But Copley had more to learn from the paintings of Joseph Blackburn, one of many wandering British portraitists who followed Smibert to the colonies in the 18th Century. Most of these artists contributed little that was original or striking to American art, but since they were fresh from London and presumably had the latest fashions at the tips of their brushes, they won the patronage of the provincials. The majority of them had come to America because they could not take the competition at home, and Blackburn, who was in and out of Boston for a decade starting around 1754, had plainly emigrated for this reason. A great deal of his work was superficial in draftsmanship and characterization, and his faces simpered; nevertheless, the poses in his portraits were unusually graceful and charming, and it was obvious that he was well acquainted with the current artistic vogue in London society. From Blackburn Copley absorbed some knowledge of artful posing, as well as some useful tricks in the rendering of jewels and laces, of shimmering silks and satins and other fine stuffs.

This, then, was the art inheritance that comprised Copley's background —the 17th Century limners, plus Smibert, Feke, Greenwood, Blackburn and a few lesser professional painters. It was not a rich background, but it was infinitely richer than Copley's later complaints to Benjamin West would make it appear. For the rest, Copley was thrown back upon his own experimenting and upon what he could glean from engravings after European artists and from books describing the old masters, their works and their ways. Of these resources, his own experimenting—begun in his childhood—was to prove the most fruitful.

Surprisingly, the earliest known example of genre painting by a native American is not a portrayal of Puritan life but a very un-Puritan scene of drunken revelry in a South American tavern. In his two-yard-long picture, *Sea Captains Carousing in Surinam,* Boston-bred John Greenwood included some New Englanders destined to figure in American history. At the large table Captain Nicholas Cooke, later governor of Rhode Island, smokes a pipe and talks with Captain Esek Hopkins, who became commander of the Continental navy. Stephen Hopkins, a future signer of the Declaration of Independence, is about to douse a companion with rum, while the artist himself, candle in hand, heads for the door.

America's First Masters

Copley was lucky to be born and raised in Boston, where the best of the small band of colonial painters lived and worked. Although his formal art training was meager, his stepfather, Peter Pelham, was a painter and engraver who perceived the boy's innate gift and took him to visit the studios of the city's leading artists. Some, like Robert Feke and John Greenwood, were American-born, while others—most notably John Smibert—were from the British Isles and had forsworn the more competitive art world of London. In their common pursuit of patronage from Boston's growing merchant class, all these men had the opportunity to study and learn from one another's work. As a result, they share some stylistic traits, either personally imported or gleaned from the reproductions of European masterworks and engravings that were available in limited quantities in the New World.

By the time Copley began his career, at the age of 15, he had a small but significant body of colonial art to inspire him. A youth of exceptional promise, he was also ambitious, and his desire for both money and social advancement led him to the profitable field of portraiture. At first, he cautiously copied the painters who had already made their names. But his abundant talent soon disclosed itself in a distinctive personal style. Before he was 21 Copley had become the finest portraitist in the colonies —and the first great artist America produced.

A mystery surrounds this portrait, which Copley painted when he was only 15. The subject has never been positively identified, but he may be Copley's stepfather, since the tools of the engraver's trade appear on the table; moreover, the painting has been in the Pelham family for five generations. While these clues point to Peter Pelham, he was dead when Copley produced the work. If the young artist was indeed memorializing his stepfather he must have worked either from another painting or from an engraving, perhaps Pelham's own self-portrait.

Peter Pelham, 1753

Peter Pelham: *The Rev. Mr. William Cooper*, 1743

The Rev. Mr. William Welsteed, 1753

Galatea Triumphs upon the Waves, engraving by Augustinus after Gregorio Lazzarini, 1700s

A gifted artist in his own right, Peter Pelham proved the perfect parent for a boy with an artistic bent. Devotedly he taught his young stepson the engraver's craft, talked to him about European art—Pelham had emigrated from London—and permitted him to pore over his art books and the many engravings he owned of English paintings. This fruitful relationship was all too brief; Pelham died only three years after his marriage to Copley's mother.

Deprived of his mentor at the age of 13, Copley did not gloomily retreat from art. Instead, he set out to master it. At first, he borrowed directly from his stepfather. In at least one case—his engraved portrait of a local cleric, the Reverend William Welsteed (*left*)—the borrowing was so extensive it would be regarded as outright plagiarism today. Copley simply appropriated an old plate of Pelham's portrait of a Reverend William Cooper (*far left*),

burnished out the head and collar and substituted Welsteed's. The fact that both subjects' names began with "Rev. William" was an added boon for Copley. He merely revised the last name in the legend below the portrait, changed the sitter's age and the date, and, in a final flourish, substituted his own name as the portraitist.

Copley also copied from Pelham's collection of engravings, although not so literally, when he turned to oil painting. One of his first efforts in this medium is based on an engraving after a painting by the 17th Century Venetian Gregorio Lazzarini, *Galatea Triumphs upon the Waves (below, left)*. It shows the mythological sea nymph raised in victory over other oceanic denizens and gods, including Poseidon with his trident. The main difference between Lazzarini's work and Copley's *(below)* is that the Italian displays Galatea stark naked while the American from puritanical Boston has discreetly draped her.

Galatea, 1754

A Quartet of Early Colonial Painters

John Smibert: *Francis Brinley,* 1731

Robert Feke: *Isaac Winslow,* c. 1748-1750

JOHN SMIBERT was the reigning painter in the colonies during Copley's boyhood. A certain blunt honesty characterized his nature as well as his art; he once explained his move from London to Boston in 1729 by saying that he would rather be a major artist in America than a minor one in England. He soon achieved his goal, winning fame by a public exhibition—America's first art show—of his painted reproductions and prints of the old masters and plaster casts of classical sculpture. Smibert's sitters were mostly local worthies like Francis Brinley (*above*). The fleshy heir of a wealthy family, Brinley is shown smugly ensconced before a panorama of Boston as seen from his Roxbury estate.

ROBERT FEKE evolved a style more elegant than Smibert's. One of the most elusive figures in American art history, Feke turned up in Boston in 1741, executed a number of increasingly sophisticated paintings apparently without benefit of formal training, and abruptly disappeared in 1750. Like his departure, his origin is also mysterious; if, as some conjecture, he was born on New York's Long Island, this would make him America's first important native painter. Feke's portraits of affluent merchants and landed gentry like Bostonian Isaac Winslow (*above*) are somewhat stiff in pose and bland in characterization, but unmatched in his time for their careful attention to the texture of rich fabrics.

John Greenwood: *Mrs. William Whipple*, c. 1752

Joseph Blackburn: *Mary Sylvester*, 1754

JOHN GREENWOOD had a virtual monopoly on the Boston portrait market after Smibert died and Feke vanished. Yet in 1752, when he was 25, he suddenly abandoned his native city and shipped out for Surinam (Dutch Guiana). The same sort of capriciousness marked his art. Greenwood's portraits are comparatively easygoing. They impressed the young Copley, who knew Greenwood as an associate of Peter Pelham's. Indeed, Copley absorbed the older artist's style so well he was long credited with the portrait of Mrs. William Whipple above. But its original touches—the sitter holding a rose to her bosom, the shy smile playing on her lips—reveal Greenwood at his buoyant best.

JOSEPH BLACKBURN, who began painting portraits in Boston in 1755, was another more sophisticated exemplar for the youthful Copley. English-born, Blackburn was far from a master, but he was adept at the fluid rococo style fashionable in 18th Century London and used it to dazzle the Yankees. For his study of Mary Sylvester *(above)*, Blackburn dressed her in the latest English mode, as a shepherdess, complete with crook. Such innovations not only won him many commissions but inspired the eager Copley to try to surpass his own more primitive efforts. So well did Copley succeed that in 1763 Blackburn left New England, probably forced out by the effective competition of his young admirer.

John Smibert: *The Bermuda Group,* 1729

Robert Feke: *The Isaac Royall Family,* 1741

John Greenwood: *The Greenwood-Lee Family,* c. 1747

The prime attraction of Smibert's Boston studio—a favorite haunt of local painters—was *The Bermuda Group (left),* a landmark in colonial art. The biggest and most ambitious group portrait yet executed in America, it memorializes an abortive expedition by the Irish-born philosopher George Berkeley and his idealistic followers to found a university in Bermuda. Berkeley stands at the right, his gaze fixed dreamily on the horizon. At the other side of the earnest group stands Smibert, his eyes coolly focused on the viewer. The painting influenced every New England artist. In a portrait of the Isaac Royall family *(top)* Feke modeled his work on Smibert's, right down to the Turkish rug covering the table. Some 18 years later Greenwood left out the rug but, like Smibert, put himself into a portrait *(above)* of his fiancée, her family—the Lees—and his mother *(second from left).*

27

Agroup portrait is, of course, more difficult to paint than the same individuals separately. Copley first faced this problem at 17, and to solve it he tapped some of his best sources of artistic inspiration. He posed the central figure in this painting as Feke did in his standing portraits, and the sitters' heads turn much like those in Greenwood's family portrait *(preceding page)*. But the young painter also employed some ideas of his own. He kept the composition less cluttered than was the custom and arranged his four figures in a simple harmonious pattern.

Less is known of the subjects of this painting than of the techniques that went into it. For want of a more specific title, the picture is called *The Brothers and Sisters of Christopher Gore*. The sitters indeed look related, but their precise identities have never been determined. The Christopher Gore of the title was not even born until about three years after this work was painted, but in time he became governor of Massachusetts and thus the portrait has acquired the title of the most illustrious member of the Gore family.

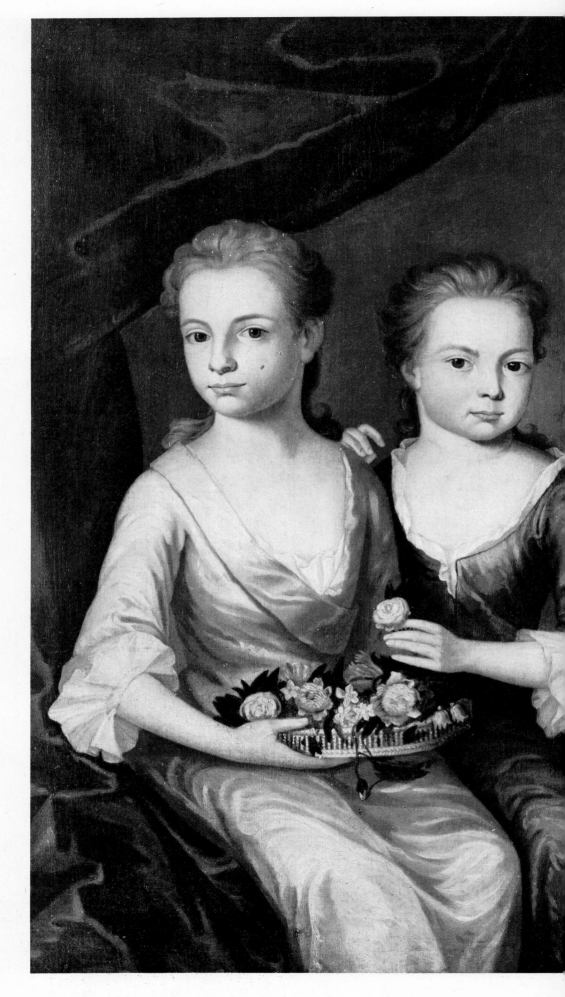

The Brothers and Sisters of Christopher Gore, c. 1755

Joseph Mann, 1754

Mrs. Joseph Mann, 175

Forced to earn a living after his stepfather died, Copley launched his career as a portraitist at the precocious age of 15. Two of his earliest efforts appear on this page. They are studies of a tavernkeeper, Joseph Mann, and his wife. Mrs. Mann's portrait reveals Copley's heavy reliance on older artists. Her wide-eyed look is reminiscent of those in portraits by Feke and Greenwood. The vague background, with its indistinct landscape and mysterious river, is also a Feke influence. Most derivative of all is Mrs. Mann's pose. It is unabashedly taken from Greenwood's Mrs. Whipple *(page 25),* which in turn was inspired by a Feke portrait, which in turn was based on an engraving of a painting of Princess Anne of England *(page 41).* Copley did try to vary Mrs. Mann's portrait from Mrs. Whipple's by reversing the position of the hands and having his sitter hold a string of pearls rather than a rose. With more success he gave some individuality to the lady's face, capturing her wistful, nervous expression. The study of her husband, produced a year later, gives evidence of Copley's growing knack for characterization, although the stiffly turned head and highlighted hands disclose a continuing debt to Greenwood's portraiture.

As Copley gained confidence and mastery, he attracted patrons more elevated than the Manns. At 17 he

Ann Tyng, 1756

Joshua Winslow, 1755

completed a portrait of Lieutenant Joshua Winslow *(above, right)*, a wealthy young Bostonian who served in Britain's colonial forces. Not yet ready to strike out entirely on his own, Copley apparently drew on Feke's portrait of Isaac Winslow *(page 24)*—no relative of Copley's sitter—for the pose of the figure and the casually exposed waistcoat. But Copley's own style also asserts itself in this work. As his subject stands proudly in his dress uniform, his cocked hat tucked under his arm, he presents a deftly characterized study in smugness. And the artist's increasingly expert eye for detail is seen in the brocade trim, lace cuffs and finely wrought ornamental

sword hilt—all rendered with handsome exactitude.

At 18 Copley was showing a new note of light sophistication in his portraits. One of his sitters, Ann Tyng *(above, left)*, was the daughter of a military officer and a member of the colonies' leading social set. Copley borrowed from Blackburn's *Mary Sylvester (page 25)* in clothing his subject in a shepherdess' gown with crook, but he gave Miss Tyng an added sheen of elegance. Although she is no great beauty, the folds of her voluminous dress, the delicate bows, and the frills of lace at her bosom and cuffs proclaim her a graceful exponent of the colonial version of English high life.

Dorothy Murray, 1759-1761

Copley's credentials as a fashionable portraitist were firmly established by the time he was 21. His study of Dorothy Murray *(above)*, the high-spirited 16-year-old daughter of a prosperous Bostonian, indicates that he was continuing to benefit from—as well as compete with —the still-popular Blackburn. Yet it also shows a further flowering of Copley's talent for capturing personality. The sly glint in Miss Murray's eye seems to say that she wants nothing more than to skip away from the sitting and slip into a more comfortable dress. Copley imitated Blackburn so well that scholars long believed the portrait of Theodore Atkinson *(opposite)* was a Blackburn opus, and one of his finest; actually, it is Copley's. Painted some two years after the Winslow portrait *(preceding page)* but more animated in pose, the study of Atkinson signals a new sureness in Copley's touch.

Theodore Atkinson, 1757-1758

Epes Sargent, 1759-1761

Copley unveiled a style completely his own in his portrait of Epes Sargent *(above)*. Sargent was a highly successful merchant, known for his outspokenness. The focus in the painting is his open, clear-eyed face *(detail opposite)* and his stubby hand, with its thick fingers fiddling at the buttons of his coat. A triumph of clarity and control, the portrait shows a new ruggedness in Copley's art, and a maturing insight into human nature. Only six years after he had set up his easel, he was the most skilled painter in colonial America.

II

Growing Up
in Boston

By the time of Copley's childhood, Boston had come a long way from
the original Puritan settlement founded in 1630. In little over a century
it had grown from a huddle of crude thatched-roof cabins into a community of nearly 15,000 people, the largest city on the North American
continent and the most important commercially.

An English traveler known only as "Mr. Bennett," visiting Boston in
1740, was impressed by what he saw and left a lively account of it.
"There are a great many good houses," he wrote, "and several fine
streets, little inferior to some of our best in London, the principal of
which is King's Street . . . at the upper end of it stands the Town House
or Guild Hall, where the Governor meets the Council and House of
Representatives; and the several courts of Justice are held there also.
And there are likewise walks for the merchants, where they meet every
day at one o'clock, in imitation of the Exchange at London, which
they call by the name of Royal Exchange too, round which are several
book-sellers' shops. . . . When the ladies ride out to take the air, it is
generally in a chaise or chair, and then but a single horse; and they
have a negro servant to drive them . . . both the ladies and gentlemen
dress and appear as gay, in common, as courtiers in England on a cor-
onation or a birthday."

Mr. Bennett also commented on the spectacle of the Long Wharf, located at the lower end of King Street (today State Street) and thrusting
2,100 feet into Boston's inner harbor. Built in 1710, it was the most dramatic structure on the city's waterfront throughout colonial times. Along
its north side was a row of shops and warehouses; along its south side
even the largest ships of the time could load and unload without the help
or expense of lighters. At Long Wharf, vessels owned by Boston merchants were freighted with such local products as dried beef and fish, fish
oil and lumber destined for other American colonies or for export abroad.
Into the merchants' warehouses came cargoes of rum, sugar, tangy spices
and exotic fruits from the West Indies, and textiles, hardware and other
manufactured goods arrived from England. As Walter Muir Whitehead
writes in his *Topographical History of Boston*, "This broad half-mile was

When Copley's widowed mother remarried in 1748, she placed the above advertisement in Boston newspapers to announce that she was continuing her late husband's tobacco business in a new location. Public notices of this kind—ranging from descriptions of runaway slaves to lost and found items—sometimes filled up to five pages in the colonial papers and cost from three to five shillings for 10 lines.

the obvious avenue to Boston from the part of the world that really mattered."

Here on the Long Wharf, a very different world from that of gay ladies and gentlemen, an Irish immigrant named Richard Copley and his wife, Mary Singleton, set up a tobacco shop in 1736. When their only child, John Singleton Copley, was born is not recorded, but most historians believe that the date was July 3, 1738. According to family tradition, the father died in the West Indies not long after, but recently discovered evidence disputes this, revealing that in 1741 he brought suit in Boston to collect a bad debt. In any case his death took place by 1748, when civic records show that the administration of his estate was granted his widow.

The inventory of worldly goods Richard Copley left is meager. One gathers from it that the family lived in three rooms over the tobacco shop —"the yellow chamber, the green chamber, and the kitchen"—and that these rooms contained a few old pieces of furniture, a few books and utensils, and precious little else. But somewhat better times awaited the widow Copley and her son. On May 22, 1748, she married Peter Pelham, an engraver and jack-of-many-trades, and moved away from the bustling, brawling waterfront to a more tranquil neighborhood. Soon after the marriage, readers of the *Boston News-Letter* were informed that "Mrs. Mary Pelham (formerly the widow Copley of the Long Wharf, Tobacconist) is removed to Lindel's Row, against the Quaker's Meeting-House, near the upper end of King Street, Boston, where she continues to sell the best Virginia Tobacco, Cut, Pigtail, and spun, of all sorts, by Wholesale, or Retail, at the Cheapest Rates."

Young John Copley's new stepfather was a remarkable character even in a city that has had more than its share of them. Born in England around 1695, Peter Pelham had been an engraver in London before coming to America in 1727. In Boston he went into partnership with another emigrant from England, the artist John Smibert; Smibert painted portraits of public figures and Pelham made engravings after these works for general sale. Such prints served much the same purpose in the 18th Century as the photographs of Presidents and astronauts sold to admirers today. Occasionally Pelham painted his own portraits of well-known Bostonians and offered prints of them for sale, and he also imported and sold engravings after European painters.

But the market for engraved portraits was limited in provincial Boston, and to make ends meet Pelham branched out. In 1732 he opened a dancing school at his house and advertised that as part of this venture he would present a monthly "assembly," or entertainment of music and dancing. This brought down on his head a thunderous denunciation in the Boston *Gazette,* so lengthy that the newspaper was constrained to publish it in two installments. The anonymous author, one suspects, was a clergyman, for the text is a choice example of the style of the old Puritan preachers whose rhetoric cannoned from every New England pulpit.

"What," exclaimed this outraged critic, "could give encouragement to so licentious and expensive a diversion in a town famous for its decency and good order? . . . When we look back upon the Transactions of our

Fore-Fathers, and read the Wonderful Story of their godly Zeal, their pious Resolution and their Publick Virtues; how should we blush and lament our present Corruption of Manners, and Decay of Religious Civic Discipline? They laid the Foundation of their Country in Piety, and a Sanctity of Life: This was Building upon a Rock . . . and Vice and Irregularities were carefully watch'd, and crop'd in the Bud. . . . But this their Posterity are too delicate to follow their sober Rules, and wise Maxims, and crying out for Music, Balls and Assemblies, like Children for their Bells and Rattles." Such frivolities, the writer concluded, were obviously "hastening the ruin of our Country, and are evils which call loudly for a Remedy."

Nevertheless, Pelham persisted in his worldly ways. In 1738 he advertised a school in which he taught "Dancing, Writing, Reading, Painting on Glass, and all sorts of needle work." Ten years later, a short time after his marriage to Mary Copley, he felt the need to supplement the earnings from his engraving trade and his bride's tobacco shop and sought public patronage for still another school. In this case the curriculum was confined to writing and arithmetic. Open "from Candle-Light till nine in the Evening . . . for the benefit of those employ'd in Business all the Day," it may well have been the first night school in America. More significant, however, was Pelham's emphasis on skills useful in business, reflecting a shift of values in the rapidly rising commercial capital of New England. Fed by the more than 500 ships a year that arrived and departed from the Long Wharf and some 40 other city quays, the mercantile spirit was more and more pervading the once-impregnable stronghold of theocratic purity.

Pelham was twice a widower when he married Mary Copley and became stepfather to her 10-year-old son. He had four sons and a daughter from his previous marriages, and at least two of the sons were then living under his roof. On February 14, 1749, he and Copley's mother had a child of their own, Henry Pelham, who was to be Copley's closest confidant throughout most of his career. With his newly acquired brothers, and away from the hectic distractions of the waterfront, young Copley probably enjoyed the same pleasures and endured the same chores as any other Boston boy of the day. No documents exist to assure us that he fished with a bent pin or went sledding on Beacon Hill, of which he was in time to own a considerable part, or that he quaked with terror as he listened to hell-fire sermons (Boston churches held services six nights a week and all day Sunday). But these are the things that history tells us every boy in colonial Boston did, and it is reasonable to assume that Copley did so too.

An education in reading, writing and arithmetic was available to him in Peter Pelham's school, right in his own home. The atmosphere was redolent of tobacco, oil paint and engraver's ink. While his mother sold "Cut, Pigtail, and spun," his stepfather worked at engraving John Smibert's portraits and now and then turned his own hand to painting. In the room of the house that Pelham used as his shop Copley and Pelham's sons were taught the engraver's trade, and there Copley saw the portraits Smibert brought to be reproduced. He also visited Smibert's studio

Soon after he arrived in Boston from England, in 1727, Peter Pelham, who later became Copley's stepfather, painted this portrait of the Reverend Cotton Mather, the ultraorthodox Puritan whose fundamentalism left a deep mark on the Massachusetts Bay Colony's way of thinking. Pelham made the picture because he needed a model for an engraving of Mather he hoped to sell; finding no likeness available, he painted one himself.

only a few streets away, with its large canvas of *The Bermuda Group* and its oil copies of paintings by Titian and other great European masters. Nor was this the only fount at which an impressionable boy could drink. There were other painters living in the neighborhood, including his stepfather's friend John Greenwood and the enigmatic Robert Feke.

This pleasant state of affairs was short-lived, however. In 1751, when Copley was 13, his stepfather died. Change also overtook the small neighborhood artists' colony. Smibert died the same year, Feke had vanished in 1750, and Greenwood left Boston for Surinam in 1752. The Pelham household remained intact for at least three years. Then it dwindled to three people: Copley, his mother and his half brother, Henry—an arrangement that lasted until Copley's marriage in 1769.

With his stepfather gone, the 13-year-old boy had to help support the family. The means were not far to seek—Peter Pelham's engraving tools and painting equipment. Copley seems to have been less interested in the former; only one engraving from his hand exists. A portrait of the Reverend Doctor William Welsteed *(page 22)*, dated 1753, it is little more than a reworking of a plate Pelham had issued 10 years earlier. It is, however, Copley's earliest known production in any medium.

Painting was obviously what fascinated him. Even as a small boy on the Long Wharf he had tried drawing, and later he had watched as his stepfather worked on his oil portraits and listened as he talked art with Smibert. But like most novices, Copley the young painter tried to run before he could walk. One of his ambitious projects was to make slightly altered oil copies of French and Italian engravings of fancy classical subjects. Three of these efforts, dated 1754, survive. One shows Galatea, the sea nymph, riding the waves in a sea-shell chariot drawn by dolphins and surrounded by other nymphs, sea horses and gods waving tridents *(page 23)*. Another shows Neptune in a similar sea chariot pulled by four terrestrial horses. In the third picture Mars, Venus and Vulcan cluster around a cauldron in which Venus is dipping arrows of love, to the transcendent delight of several cupids. Although the anatomy is crude and the perspective poor, these early Copley works are playful and marked by a distinctive sweetness of color—qualities which, unknown to Copley, were features of the decorative Rococo style then in vogue in Europe. For all the realism that characterized his later paintings, Copley was ultimately to emerge as the leading colonial exponent of the Rococo style.

When he started out, however, he was quick to realize that there was not much market in Boston for fancy classical themes and that Bostonians valued art primarily as a means of recording likenesses. So even while producing his Nereids, nymphs and gods he turned to the painting of portraits.

There were several reasons why he decided that he would paint rather than engrave them. By 18th Century esthetic standards, painting was Art with a capital A, but engraving was merely a trade. Copley knew this from reading the few treatises on art that Peter Pelham had owned, including Count Francesco Algarotti's *Letters upon Painting* and Daniel Webb's *An Inquiry into the Beauties of Painting*. More philosophical than technical, these books so impressed Copley that he was still referring to them in letters he wrote as a mature man. He seems to have been particularly impressed by their glorification of painting above all other arts and of High Renaissance masters above all other artists. While portrait painting was regarded as the lowest step on the stairway to artistic Parnassus, it *was* a step. Perhaps, after making one's reputation with portraits in provincial Boston, one could go to Europe, see the works of the old masters at first hand and then paint the grand themes—historical, religious, mythological—which all the books agreed were the pinnacle of the painter's art.

Another persuasive argument in favor of painting portraits as against engraving them was the greater gain it promised. Then, as in his later years when he had become famous and prosperous, economic security was a matter of intense concern to Copley. In Boston the people who could afford oil portraits were the government officials, civic leaders and wealthy merchants. They not only had the money to pay for the most expensive likenesses but suitable settings in which to display them. There was, for example, the mansion of Sir Charles Henry Frankland, who had been sent from London to serve as collector of the port. The house had 26 rooms, a stairway so wide Frankland reportedly could ride his pony up it, paneled parlors with fluted columns and gilded cornices, and, everywhere, mantelpieces of the finest Italian marble. To adorn such mantels with mere engravings would never do. On the other hand, learning to paint pictures appropriate to mansions would take time, endless experimentation and unremitting effort.

Young Copley, however, was willing and eager on all scores, and thus was formed a personality fiercely dedicated in its industry, coolly calculating in its ambition and ever alert to the main chance. The progressively affluent status of Copley's sitters is a good index of what a modern sociologist would call his "upward mobility."

Princess Anne, the daughter of James II, was crowned Queen of England in 1702 and died in 1714. She never visited the colonies, but she could lay claim to being an important influence on American art because an engraved portrait of her *(above)* was used as a model by no fewer than four noted American painters. The first to do so, John Smibert, used her pose in his own portraits of two ladies. Robert Feke adapted one of Smibert's variations. John Greenwood's version is shown on page 25; Copley's is seen on page 30.

The climb upward began modestly enough, however, with a portrait of a baker's daughter and tavernkeeper's wife, Mrs. Joseph Mann *(page 30)*. Produced in 1753, when Copley was 15, it is not only his earliest known painting but also one of his few fully signed and dated works. Perhaps adolescent self-pride alone prompted this gesture; perhaps there was another motivation as well. Pelham and Smibert were dead, Feke had disappeared, and John Greenwood had recently departed for Surinam. Copley may have decided to affix his signature and the date as a deliberate bench mark, to signalize the start of an independent career in art.

Copley's genius for capturing the essence of character is already manifest, although only in embryonic form, in his portrayal of Mrs. Mann's snub nose and broad, short chin; these are the nose and chin of Bethia Torrey Mann and of nobody else. But the rest of the picture is a mass of borrowings. Mrs. Mann wears precisely the same style of blue dress with white ruffles at the sleeves and neck that Smibert used over and over again in his portraits of women, and the curls cascading over her shoulders are also Smibertian. Her placid face, with its widely separated eyes, reveals an indebtedness to Feke. Her seated pose and her gesture of fingering a string of pearls are adapted from an old engraving from which

Shipped to the colonies, engravings of fashionable English portraits provided Copley with elegant models for his own commissions; indeed, his sitters probably chose the pose and costume they liked best from a variety of prints the painter showed them. Above is an engraving of a portrait of Lady Caroline Russell painted by Joshua Reynolds in London about 1759. Below is Copley's portrait of a matron from the Boston area, painted in the late 1760s.

Smibert, Feke and Greenwood had all previously borrowed—a likeness of Britain's Princess (later Queen) Anne. Like his predecessors, Copley tried to hide the origin of the pose by altering and simplifying details; among other things, he substituted a rather crudely painted river in the background for the castle in the Princess Anne engraving. His attempts at concealment were unsuccessful; the liny, angular way in which he painted the folds of Mrs. Mann's dress plainly betrays the picture's source in an engraving.

Although today such borrowings would be considered outright plagiarism, in Copley's time the concept of property rights in artistic composition was not yet widespread. The 18th Century art world frankly embraced a principle later expressed by the writer James Branch Cabell, that a builder who wishes to erect a permanent structure uses seasoned timbers. Thus English engravings, as a source of stylistic traits and specific imagery, were to exert an important influence on Copley's work throughout his Boston years. As his art matured, he relied on them less and less. Nevertheless it comes as a shock to discover that his portrait of Mrs. Jerathmael Bowers, painted about 15 years after Mrs. Mann's and apparently a masterpiece of originality in Copley's most advanced American style, actually follows in minute detail an engraving after Joshua Reynolds.

In fairness, it should be pointed out that Copley may have imitated engravings at the specific behest of his sitters. Among modish colonials, English prints were widely regarded as mirrors of fashion, and were imported by the bundle. But in any event, soon after Copley launched his career some of his portraits began to show less dependence on engravings and more on the ideas of the newly arrived British painter, Joseph Blackburn. With Blackburn's appearance on the Boston scene in 1755, Copley was exposed to the work of a man with recent, firsthand knowledge of London's fads and furbelows and also of Europe's increasingly popular Rococo style. Soon Copley's portraits reflected Blackburn's graceful poses and his expert handling of elegant accessories, particularly the way he imparted richness to textiles.

Copley's indebtedness to Blackburn notably appears in his 1756 portrait of Ann Tyng (page 31), the daughter of a commodore in the British Navy and the bride-to-be of a British Army officer. Taking over a convention which Blackburn had introduced to America in his portrait of Mary Sylvester Deering (page 25), Copley painted his subject as a rococo shepherdess, complete with crook and lamb, in a pastoral landscape. Blackburn's influence is also evident in the care lavished on Ann Tyng's white silk dress, red cloak, blue ribbons and lace ruffles—a great improvement over Copley's unconvincing treatment of Mrs. Mann's drapery three years earlier. But Ann Tyng also shows signs that Copley was now beginning to strike out on his own; her face is far more individual than any of his earlier known portraits, and in general the 18-year-old artist's effort is more realistic than any work by the older and more experienced Blackburn.

By the time he was 20, Copley had produced about 40 portraits. They document not only the astonishing speed with which he was mastering his craft, but his steady progression up the social ladder as well. From portraying a tavernkeeper's wife in 1753 to a commodore's daughter in 1756, he had reached the point where his services were in demand by the loftiest members of New England's moneyed society. His acceptance was signaled, in particular, by a double likeness he was commissioned to produce around 1758.

His subjects were Mary and Elizabeth Royall, the daughters of one of New England's wealthiest citizens. Isaac Royall owned extensive lands in Massachusetts, Maine and the West Indies. His estate at Medford, near Boston, included a palatial house, vast gardens, stables and quarters for 27 slaves. In time he was destined to have to forgo these comforts. As a leading Tory—one of the supporters of the British Crown who opposed the independence-minded Whigs during the American Revolution —Royall went to England at the outbreak of the war and thus suffered the confiscation of his American properties; his Medford estate, still preserved today *(pages 46-57),* is an impressive testimonial to the luxurious living possible in 18th Century New England.

Copley's painting of the Royall sisters *(page 36)* shows them in blue and white silk dresses, sitting in a veritable lava flow of red velvety material, with an additional rivulet of orange between them. At the same time the faces of the two attractive youngsters are more firmly characterized than any of Copley's portraits to date. Not long after producing this work, he began to hit his stride as a major artist. By about the year 1760 he had very nearly attained the remarkable degree of realism and the penetrating characterization that mark his finest portraits. These qualities pervade *Epes Sargent (pages 34-35)* and *Dorothy Murray (page 32),* both painted around this time. In each case the individual transcends the type. Sargent, heavy, middle-aged, a successful merchant and shipowner of Gloucester and a staunch Whig, has the argumentative look of the endless talker he was (it was not for nothing that Gloucester made him its representative to the Massachusetts assemblies). His fleshy right hand fiddles with his coat, seeming to button and unbutton it. This apparently inconsequential gesture heralds an important feature of Copley's mature art; it was in such touches that he began to show his unique gift for observing unconscious personal mannerisms—the way people fuss with their clothes, feel their faces, or tap on tables to emphasize a point. Master portraitist that he was, Copley was instinctively aware that a characteristic gesture or attitude could individualize a portrait more dramatically than such external details as the elaborate architectural settings he sometimes used to proclaim a sitter's station in life.

Every bit as much a personality as Epes Sargent is 16-year-old Dorothy Murray. This Boston belle, standing ramrod straight in her golden-brown dress, holding a wreath of magnificently painted flowers, seems as solemn as a Spanish princess by Velázquez. Yet for all her gravity a mischievous look in her eyes betrays her spirited nature. Both in her face and stance Copley caught a certain determination that was to be amply confirmed later at the time of the Revolution. To harbor a number of Tories who could not flee the country, Dorothy turned her aunt's farm at

Milton, near Boston, into a refuge for them and successfully avoided efforts by Revolutionary forces to confiscate the property.

How much Copley was paid for the Sargent or Murray commissions, or for his other portraits done around the same time, is unrecorded. In any event, in his growing zeal for self-advancement he decided to add two side lines. One was the painting of miniatures on copper and ivory, intended more as keepsakes than as likenesses. The other was a less expensive type of portraiture than oils, pastels; the materials were cheaper, less time was involved in turning out the product, and more customers were likely to be attracted. Copley had already produced a few pastels, but in evident dissatisfaction with the materials available to him he drafted a letter in September of 1762 to the Swiss artist Jean-Étienne Liotard, who then enjoyed an international reputation as a pastelist. The letter is interesting less for the request it made than for its revelation of Copley's restless state of mind. After asking Liotard to send him "one sett of Crayons of the very best kind such as You can recommend [for] liveliness of colour and Justness of tints," he added: "You may perhaps be surprised that so remote a corner of the Globe as New England should have any d[e]mand for the necessary eutensils for practiceing the fine Arts, but I assure You Sir however feeble our efforts may be, it is not for want of inclination that they are not better, but the want of opportunity to improve ourselves. however America which has been the seat of war and desolation, I would fain hope will one Day become the school of fine Arts and Monsieur Liotard['s] drawings with Justice be set as patterns for our imitation. not that I have ever had the advantage of beholding any one of those rare pieces from Your hand, but [I have] formed a Judgment on the true tast[e] of several of My friend[s] who has seen em."

It is not known whether Liotard ever received this letter and complied with Copley's request—or, indeed, whether the letter was ever sent. (It was unearthed in 1914 in a collection of Copley family papers, long forgotten in London's Public Record Office.) But the fact that the letter was written at all is evidence of the way Copley constantly reached out to improve his craftsmanship during his formative period. And the respect it implied for Europe's art, the sense of isolated deprivation it expressed, were to recur in his correspondence for the rest of his years in America.

With or without help from Liotard, Copley continued to create his pastel portraits, ultimately producing some that rank among the best of the 18th Century, an era of great popularity for this medium. Smaller than his oils, they are also devoid of accessories and the sitter is seen close up. Copley may have decided to add pastels to his line of pictorial goods for reasons beyond the merely economic. Since the technique of pastel lies halfway between the techniques of drawing and painting, he may have welcomed the exercise the medium afforded. When painting in oils he and his New England predecessors seem to have started their work directly on the canvas, without making a preliminary sketch; not a single drawing by Smibert, Feke or Blackburn is known to exist, only one or two by Greenwood survive, and Copley's early drawings—all of them produced at the very outset of his career—can be counted on the fingers of one hand. Copley may also have enjoyed the change that pastel offered in scale and range of colors.

Interestingly, he chose this medium, rather than oils, when he portrayed himself for the first time, in 1769. Somewhat like an architect who commissions a colleague to build his house because he cannot afford to execute his own best ideas, Copley may have made this choice purely out of thrift. The picture shows him as a square-faced, serious man of 31, wearing a gray-powdered wig, a richly embroidered waistcoat, and over it the same sort of brocaded dressing gown favored by the Boston tycoons whose portraits he was now producing in increasing numbers.

B y the time of the self-portrait, Copley was well entrenched as the leading portrait painter in Boston, and his reputation had spread far beyond it. From New York, from Philadelphia, from Canada, letters came asking for sittings and even proposing that he pull up stakes and venture into new territory.

He had received one such letter from a satisfied sitter, Thomas Ainslie, as early as 1764. From his home in Quebec Ainslie wrote urging that Copley travel north to explore the Canadian market for portraits. His own, he reported, had had a special sort of success. He had sent it across the Atlantic to his parents' home in Glasgow. There it was seen by his 15-month-old son, on a visit. The child's reaction, as relayed in a letter by his grandfather to Ainslie, had been extraordinary; when "the Infant eyed your Picture, he spring to it, roared, and schriched, and attempted gripping the hand, but when he could not catch hold of it, nor gett You to speak to him, he stamp'd and scolded, and when any of us askt him for Papa, he always turned and pointed to the Picture. What think you of his proof of the Painters Skill in taking Your likeness?"

Ainslie's retelling of all this drew a gratified response from Copley. It gave him, he noted, "no small pleasure to receive the approbation of so uncorrupted a judgment as that of so Young a Child." But as to Ainslie's proposal that he come to Quebec for portrait painting, he wrote: "I should receive a singular pleasure in excepting if my Business was in any ways slack, but it is so far otherwise that I have a large Room full of Pictures unfinished, which would ingage me these twelve months, if I did not begin any others; this renders it impossible for me to leave the place I am in. . . . I assure You I have been as fully imployed these several Years past as I could expect or wish to be, as more would be a means to retard the design I have always had in vew, that of improveing in that charming Art which is my delight and gaining a reputation rather than a fortune. Tho if I could obtain the one while in the persuit of the other, I confess I should [be] so far from being indiferent about either that I would willingly use great diligence for the acquireing of both."

At the time of this writing Copley's reputation was already secure, and the groundwork for his fortune was well laid. But he had one yearning yet to fulfill. Increasingly he had begun to feel that approval by his fellow Americans was not a true gauge of an artist's worth. He hungered for recognition abroad. The means by which he achieved this goal was a portrait of his half brother, Henry Pelham. Its exhibition in London in 1766 marked the Great Divide of Copley's career.

A Patron's Show Place

Copley's stature as a portraitist gave him access to some of the finest homes in and around Boston. One of the most elegant, five miles from the city, in Medford, belonged to Isaac Royall Jr. The three-story, 12-room mansion was built by Colonel Isaac Royall Sr., who had spent most of his life on the island of Antigua in the West Indies, where he amassed a fortune as a plantation owner, a sugar and rum trader and slave merchant. The colonel —himself the son of a carpenter and grandson of a cooper —died in 1739, shortly after moving into the Medford house, and for the next 36 years his son lived in a world of grandeur and lavish entertainments perhaps unrivaled in colonial New England.

Copley's association with the Royall family—he painted portraits of Royall, his wife and their daughters —apparently left an indelible mark on him. Born to a poor tobacconist, Copley yearned to improve his social standing, and the Royalls' own rapid rise proved it could be done. But Isaac Royall's tasteful way of life ended as the Revolution drew near. He abandoned Royall House in 1775, went to Halifax in Canada and there took ship for England. During the war he tried to reclaim his property but failed. It changed hands several times during the 19th Century and, in 1908, was purchased and restored by a group of history-minded New Englanders banded together as the Royall House Association, which maintains the place today.

For the western façade of Royall House Isaac Royall wanted to re-create the handsome stonework of English Georgian architecture. But he wished to use wood instead of stone, perhaps because skilled carpenters were more readily available than stonemasons. So he hired craftsmen to simulate a stone-block façade. Also made of wood are the curved pediment and fluted Ionic pilasters of the doorway, which faced the gardens.

Photographed by Robert Walch

The front hall of Royall House, which bisects it, reflects the neoclassical architectural style that was especially popular in 18th Century England. Called Georgian after the English kings of the period, it is seen in the archway and staircase that dominate the hall. The archway's keystone and Corinthian capitals (*detail above*), as well as the balusters of the staircase, were carved and hand-turned by the best craftsmen of the day. The staircase, whose 18 steps were so well proportioned that little effort was needed to ascend them, features an intricately carved newel (*right*) and a handrail made of a single piece of mahogany.

The wallpaper in the hall, not original to the house but added later, was printed from authentic wood blocks of the era. It is Chinese in motif and reflects the interest in Far Eastern decoration that was sparked both in Europe and America by the opening up of trade with the Orient.

The west parlor of Royall House was used for the entertainment of guests or, at more informal times, for the diversion of the ladies of the house. They found the recessed window seats ideal hideaways in which to relax over their needlework and hold tête-à-têtes. In addition, their parlor nooks provided good views of the gardens of the estate, which may possibly have included a maze of carefully cut hedges in the European fashion of the day.

Although the furniture in the room today was not originally in the house, it is similar to the superb collection of pieces Isaac inherited from his father. The walnut Queen Anne side chair by the window was made about 1730. The Chippendale sofa dates from 1760. The chaise longue above, also from the Queen Anne period, is upholstered in needlework produced in 1735. Copley's portraits of Royall and his family may have been hung in this room, although not one of them remains in the house today.

Called the "Marble Chamber," the generously proportioned room at right was the bedroom of the master of Royall House. When the property was confiscated during the Revolution, this room was used by one of Washington's colonels for conferences during the siege of Boston in 1775. The chamber's name came from the Corinthian pilasters—flanking the fireplace and archways—that itinerant craftsmen painted to look like marble. The fireplace itself, lined with English tiles and topped by a pastoral painting, was constantly attended by Royall's slaves during the winter, but as added protection against the New England cold the windows in the room —as well as those in the rest of the house—were kept firmly shuttered. The wallpaper now in the Marble Chamber re-creates the original, which was made of Spanish leather with Chinese overpainting. The woodwork was green, and crimson damask was used for upholstery as well as for the bedspread and draperies. The photograph above shows part of another bedroom, with a cozy four-poster. Curtained canopy beds of this type were intended not so much for privacy as for warmth.

In winter months servants prepared the Royall family's meals—as well as fare for the frequent banquets for guests —in the kitchen *(left)*. When warm weather came, the cooking was moved to the slave quarters to keep disagreeable odors and oppressive heat out of the main house. The spartan look of the kitchen contrasts sharply with the elegance of the wainscoted dining room above. Suspended over a Queen Anne table, the brass chandelier is a reproduction of a Flemish design popular in the mid-18th Century. Copley may have dined here with his patron. Such surroundings helped whet his appetite for the gracious living only men like Royall could afford.

The east façade
of Royall House.

III

A Transatlantic Triumph

To prove himself by London's demanding art standards Copley painted this portrait of his half brother, Henry Pelham. As was usual in portraits of children, Copley included a pet animal. In this case it is a flying squirrel, so called because the broad membrane between its hind and fore legs enables it to glide between trees in its nocturnal hunts for food. A sociable creature, it was a popular pet in colonial households.

Boy with a Squirrel, 1765
(see color detail on slipcase)

Without realizing it, Copley chose a good time to make his bid for recognition in London. When he submitted his first entry to an exhibition there in 1766, public showings of art were still a novelty in the English capital. Several societies of artists were competing for popular attention, and in characteristic 18th Century fashion witty pamphleteers were having a field day over the rivalries of the various groups. Moreover, since no serious tension yet existed between the mother country and the American colonies, the nationalistic pride of both the societies and the critics readily extended to the work of young colonial painters. To many they represented a pure British strain untainted by Continental influences, an attitude that had already contributed to the sensational success in England of Pennsylvania-born Benjamin West.

Traditionally the viewing of works of art had been the privilege only of private collectors. The idea of exhibiting to the public had largely originated with William Hogarth. In 1740 the great painter of contemporary manners and mores, whose satirical outlook on life concealed a broad humanitarian streak, gave London's Foundling Hospital his portrait of Captain Thomas Coram, the philanthropic shipbuilder who had recently established this home for unwanted infants. Hogarth's motive was not entirely selfless, however. He knew that the painting would be seen there by many more people than could view it in his studio. Other artists took his cue and began donating works to the Hospital, and in time its board of governors was composed entirely of painters and sculptors.

In 1759 the board met to consider the notion of an annual exhibition of new paintings, and the following year put on London's first public art showing. It ran for two weeks, with a daily attendance of more than 1,000, in quarters in the Strand owned by the ambitiously named Royal Society of Arts for the Encouragement of Arts, Manufactures, and Commerce. Soon jealousies and conflicts split the exhibiting artists into two rival organizations. The more important, the Society of Artists of Great Britain, counted among its founding members Hogarth, Joshua Reynolds, the most sought-after portrait painter in London, and Thomas Gainsborough. This new group, in turn, held its first public showing in an auction room at Spring Gardens—in the heart of London—in 1761. The spirit of the event was caught in Hogarth's tailpiece to the catalogue, a sketch of a monkey dressed as a dandy watering dead plants marked "Exoticks." Hogarth was saying, in effect, that the English connoisseur's long-standing bias for Continental art was doomed, and that native English art was coming into its own at last. A letter to a newspaper of the day made this point explicitly. It told of a young country squire who had been invited by his London host to "come with me and help me to despise the wretched English daubs at Spring Gardens." But the countryman, with his uncorrupted British taste, found the show wonderful and Hogarth's monkey a perfect portrayal of his foppish host. (Hogarth, whose loathing for foreign art was well known, was not above composing this letter himself.)

Success continued to attend the yearly exhibits of the Society of Artists of Great Britain, and by 1763 it had 60 members and enough self-esteem to launch the ritual of an annual dinner. The first, given at the Turk's Head Tavern, featured "Cods' Heads and Sauce, Stewed Carp, Soles and Whitings; Ox Head, Marrow Pudding, Fowls, Geese, Veal Pie, Salad, Beefsteak Pie, Greens and Carrots, and Fried Soles and Ham" —all washed down with wine and tankards of porter. Two years later the Society was granted a royal charter and added the word "Incorporated" to its name.

It was at its exhibition of 1766 that Copley was introduced to the London public. His entry, *Boy with a Squirrel,* has the distinction of being, so far as anyone knows, the first picture painted in America to be exhibited abroad. Copley had shipped it to an American friend then residing in London, a sea captain named R. G. Bruce. Evidently Bruce was a staunch admirer of Copley's work; it may even have been his idea to test London's reaction to the Bostonian's art. In any event, the captain took the painting to Lord Buchan, a noted connoisseur, who in turn brought it to the attention of Joshua Reynolds, who arranged for its showing at Spring Gardens.

Boy with a Squirrel (page 58 and slipcase) is a portrait of Copley's half brother, Henry Pelham. He sits at a polished mahogany table with a red drape behind him. A pet squirrel, held on a gold chain, perches on the table eating a nut; nearby is a glass of water. The elements of the composition are simple, but deceptively so. Every one of them is intended to emphasize the range of Copley's gifts: his fidelity to life, his flair for color, his skill at textures, his mastery of such difficult tricks as rendering the minor gleam of a tabletop or the translucence of a water glass. While demonstrating his virtuosity, moreover, Copley wisely kept to well-established tradition: from time immemorial, animals have appeared in portraits of children, as much a convention as an arrow piercing a seminaked male figure signifies a portrayal of St. Sebastian. Curiously, Pelham himself was no longer a child when Copley painted the portrait in 1765; he was actually 16. *Boy with a Squirrel* was doubtless based on an extraordinarily free, rather smoky oil sketch—Copley's only known work in this technique—that he had made of his half brother around 1758, when the sitter was nine.

Beyond question, Copley created *Boy with a Squirrel* with the deliberate intent of using it as an exhibition piece; it may have been the first painting so conceived in America. The critical reaction to its appearance in London proved that his calculation had paid off. The reviewer for the *London Chronicle* described Copley's entry as "very clever," and added: "I am told it is the production of a young artist, if so, with proper application there is no doubt of his making a good painter." Another critic, with the pseudonym "An Impartial Hand," hailed Copley as "a young laurel that shall reach the skies." Manifestly, the London climate was ripe for talented Americans; the same critic waxed positively poetic over another colonial exhibitor, Benjamin West:

> West and genius met me at the door . . .
> Thou long expected, wish'd for Stranger, hail!
> In Britain's bosom make thy loved abode
> And open daily to her raptured Eye
> The mystic wonders of the Raphael's school

More good news was in store for Copley in the reaction of the English artistic fraternity. In August of 1766, two months after the exhibition closed, he heard from Captain Bruce that *Boy with a Squirrel* "was universally allowed to be the best Picture of its kind that appeared on that occasion." Correctly assuming that Copley would be particularly eager for the opinion of Joshua Reynolds, Bruce candidly reported that the great man had found certain faults in Copley's picture—"a little hardness in the drawing, Coldness in the shades. An over minuteness." But on the whole Reynolds' verdict could not have been more gratifying. Not only did he think the picture better than any portrait Benjamin West had ever done, but, Bruce reported, "he did not know one Painter at home, who had all the Advantages that Europe could give them, that could equal it, and that if you are capable of producing such a Piece by the mere Efforts of your own Genius, with the advantages of the Example and Instruction which you could have in Europe, You would be a valuable Acquisition to the Art, and one of the first Painters in the World provided you could receive these Aids before it was too late in Life, and before your Manner and Taste were corrupted or fixed by working in your little way at Boston." Reynolds' conclusion, as relayed by Bruce, was: "It is a wonderful Picture to be sent by a Young Man who was never out of New England, and had only some bad Copies to study."

Bruce also informed Copley that while Joshua Reynolds himself was too busy to give him personal counsel on painting, Benjamin West was willing to help instead. And since "the Friends of your Art" wanted Copley to exhibit again the next year, West had promised to point out a suitable subject.

The proffered assistance took the form of a letter that accompanied Bruce's. West (one of the world's great orthographic individualists even in an era of free and easy spelling) observed among other things that when Copley's picture was first "Excibited to View, the Criticizems was that at first Sight the Picture struck the Eye as being to[o] liney, which was judged to have arose from there being so much neetness in the lines." For the next year's exhibition, he suggested that Copley "Paint a Picture of a half figure or two in one Piec, of a Boy and Girle, or any other subject you may fance . . . and don't trust any resemblac of any thing to[o] fancey, except the disposition of they figures and they adjustment of draperies. So as to make an agreeable whole." Like Reynolds, West felt that Copley should come to Europe as soon as possible.

Elated at the reception of *Boy with a Squirrel,* and at the knowledge that he could now count on sophisticated advice from abroad, Copley was further delighted by a letter a month later. It informed him that he had been elected a member of the Incorporated Society of Artists of Great Britain and requested him to appear at the Turk's Head Tavern on the evening of October 6, 1766, for his formal induction. Much as he may have wanted to, Copley could not just pick up and go. He had portrait commissions in Boston that demanded all his time and energy, and he was also fearful of risking the financial security he now enjoyed. But the invitation no doubt directed his dreams all the more firmly toward the time when he would cross the Atlantic and "be heated with the sight of the enchanting works of a Raphael, a Rubens, a Coregio, a Veronese."

Copley did not follow West's suggestion that for next year's show he paint "a half figure or two in one Piec." A full-length portrait, he decided, would present a greater challenge. The resulting picture turned out to be a kind of paraphrase of *Boy with a Squirrel.* It portrayed a little girl on her knees before an upholstered chair, playing with a parrot while a dog looks on.

London's enthusiastic reception of his *Boy with a Squirrel* in 1766 spurred Copley to exhibit a second picture there the next year. Five months after shipping *Young Lady with a Bird and Dog* (sometimes known as *Mary Warner*), the Bostonian learned the critics' verdict: the painting was not up to England's sophisticated standards. The desire to improve his art to meet those standards eventually led Copley to go abroad to study.

Again the faithful Captain Bruce reported from London. From the standpoint of execution, he wrote, some critics felt that *Young Lady with a Bird and Dog* (now known as *Mary Warner*) outshone all other pictures in the 1767 exhibit. But, he added, "you have been universally condemned in the choice of your Subject, which is so disagreable a Character, as to have made the Picture disliked by every one but the best Judges who could discern the Excellence of the Painting." As for Reynolds, said the captain, he approved of Copley's wonderfully correct draftsmanship but also "exclaimed against the Subject." The letter ended encouragingly, however, assuring Copley that "the Artists depend on another Exhibition from You next Year. They already put you on a footing with all the Portrait Painters except Mr. Reynolds. If You have been able to attain this unassisted at Boston, What might you not achieve in Europe?"

Reynolds' criticism was echoed and amplified by West: "The General Affect . . . is not so agreable in this as in the other which arrises from Each Part of the Picture being Equell in Strength of Coulering and finishing, Each Making to[o] much a Picture of it. . . . Your Picture is in Possession of Drawing to a Correctness that is very Surpriseing, and of Coulering very Briliant, tho this Briliantcy is Somewhat missaplyed, as for instance, the Gown is too bright for the flesh, which over Came it in Brilency. This made them Critisise, they Shadows of the Flesh . . . and so in like manner the dog and Carpet to[o] Conspichious for Excesery things." Again West urged Copley to come abroad to see "the great Productions of art, and feel from them what words Cannot Express . . . and if you should Ever Come to London my house is at Your Service."

Why a picture of a little girl with a dog and parrot should have been so generously damned on grounds of subject matter is difficult to understand today; possibly the Londoners were put off by a certain bluntness of presentation in the painting. Less difficult to appreciate are the stylistic criticisms of West. The defects of one era often become the virtues of another, and our own time relishes precisely the same equality of emphasis in a painting that struck West and his contemporaries as a serious flaw. The 20th Century believes, as Henri Matisse once put it, that every part of a picture must work as hard as every other part.

The cool reception given Copley's second exhibition piece made it obvious to him that in order to become a truly great painter by European standards he would have to heed West's urging to come to Europe to study its masterpieces at first hand. But still he hesitated to make that momentous decision. "I am in as good business as the poverty of this place will admit," he wrote to Captain Bruce in the fall of 1767. "I make as much as if I were a Raphael or a Correggio; and three hundred guineas a year, my present income, is equal to nine hundred in London." He might chafe at local tastes, which confined him to the painting of portraits while visions of great canvases full of historic and religious subjects danced in his head, but portraits brought him monetary rewards he was by no means sure of matching in Europe. He was not yet ready to hazard crossing the Atlantic.

For several years he painted no more pictures for London, concentrating instead on the improvement of what Reynolds had called "your little way." He had already begun to enrich that "little way" with a number of mannerisms even before the success of *Boy with a Squirrel,* and they were to give Copley's work a strong individuality throughout his remaining American years.

For example, in his frequent portrayals of merchants and lawyers at home in informal dress, he almost invariably showed them working with books or accounts at draped tables. Often he marshaled the light in such a way as to suggest that the viewer of the picture had just entered the room, throwing a sheet of illumination on the figure at the table. Sometimes the sitter looks up quizzically at the viewer, as if to ask what brought him there. Copley painted one wealthy Boston merchant, Nicholas Boylston *(page 85),* no fewer than three times in this casual attitude; the various versions, all done around 1767, were apparently intended for members of Boylston's family and for Harvard College, of which he was an important benefactor. Boylston, it seems, was unstinting in his own behalf as well. John Adams, the future President and then a law student in Boston, confided to his diary: "Dined at Mr. Nick Boylstones. An elegant dinner indeed! Went over the House to view the Furniture, which alone cost a thousand Pounds sterling. A Seat it is for a noble man, a Prince. The Turkey Carpets, the painted Hangings, the Marble Tables, the rich Beds with crimson Damask Curtains and Counterpanes, the beautiful Chimney Clock, the Spacious Garden, are the most magnificent of any thing I have ever seen."

Along with his informal seated portraits of prominent Bostonians, Copley began to portray them full length, in imaginary architectural settings

Shortly after his marriage in November 1769 to Susanna Farnham Clarke, daughter of a wealthy Boston merchant, Copley made these pastel sketches of his bride and himself. With his marriage and increasing fame and fortune, Copley could justify doing a self-portrait on the grounds that he had now achieved the same social standing and financial success as many of his patrons.

intended to heighten the impressiveness of their image. Thomas Hancock, uncle of the first signer of the Declaration of Independence, dealt in paper, codfish, whale oil, molasses, rum, tea and sailcloth. His ego must have been well served when Copley painted him standing amid sundry pieces of carved and upholstered furniture in a great classically inspired rotunda. Nathaniel Sparhawk *(page 82),* whose commercial activities were no less extensive than Hancock's and who was a distinguished judge to boot, appeared in equally grandiose surroundings that featured immense fluted columns, a staircase adorned with a huge urn and a garden entered through a high ornamental arch.

One turns with relief from such lords of creation to Copley's little old ladies. From about 1765 on he tended to portray them in much the same pose—seated in brocade-upholstered chairs. Some critics would have us believe that Copley's paintings of little old ladies were especially sympathetic because they offered him no disconcerting challenges, as younger women might. But the sympathy is, in fact, modern. We, today's viewers, happen to like Copley's old ladies because they do not indulge in showy excesses of costume, pose or architectural adornment.

Another Copley mannerism that became increasingly evident in his portraits of women, both old and young, was his charming way of showing them hospitably proffering fruit or thoughtfully leaning on one hand. Sometimes they appear in a simple head-and-shoulders pose, sometimes in a more elaborately orchestrated composition with accessories. But always the aim and achievement of these paintings is a warm and vital realism; the portrait of Nicholas Boylston's mother *(page 77)* is a notable example. As John Adams observed of Copley's mature likenesses of both women and men, "You can scarcely help discoursing with them, asking questions and receiving answers."

None of these portraits was painted without plodding, slogging labor. Copley was no slapdash virtuoso. At the height of his productivity in America, between 1762 and 1770, he averaged two pictures a month, but he had been nearly 10 years arriving at that tempo, and after 1770 his output gradually declined to about 18 portraits a year.

Many of the paintings of his most prolific period were of prominent New England Tories, those loyal supporters of the British Crown who had the wherewithal and status to command his services. Apparently Copley also associated with them socially, for on November 17, 1769, he married the daughter of loyalist Richard Clarke, one of Boston's richest merchants and local agent for the British East India Company, whose powerful trading monopoly Parliament itself had sanctioned. How Copley first met Susanna Farnham Clarke is not known. Evidently it was not a portrait commission that brought them together; Copley did not paint her or any member of her family until well after his marriage, although he did produce a pastel of his attractive bride sometime shortly after their wedding.

Their union was destined to last 45 years, and to produce six children, three of whom, like their mother, lived into their nineties. Susanna Copley —her husband called her "Sukey"—seems to have been quiet and self-effacing. The many letters she wrote in later years in England reveal her as a warm and devoted woman deeply interested in Copley's work. The letters, published in 1882 by her granddaughter, Martha Babcock Amory, in an eminently Victorian book, *The Domestic and Artistic Life of John Singleton Copley, R.A.*, are full of intimate family chitchat, but they also refer to various episodes in Copley's stormy English career and they do so with a staunchly loyal bias.

England, however, was still only a glimmer in Copley's mind at the time of his marriage. Soon afterward he began to buy property on Beacon Hill, then an almost completely rural part of Boston. He called his land a "farm" and named it Mount Pleasant. The property, which adjoined that of John Hancock, ultimately included 20 acres. It ran all the way to the Charles River and embraced all of what is now Louisburg Square. Mount Pleasant was to cause Copley endless trouble, first because of litigation over the title to the land, then because of bickering with the contractor over extensive reconstructions that the artist ordered on the three houses on the property. As a result the Copleys did not take up residence—in the largest of the remodeled houses—until 1772.

Copley's "great house" no longer stands on Beacon Hill, but his agreement with the contractor survives to give some idea of what it was like. The main part of the structure was two stories high, with a small lookout and a "neat Chinese Tarret" crowning the shingle roof. In the entrance hall, a staircase with a twist rail led upstairs. Among other features were a parlor reserved for special occasions, a sitting room for everyday use and four bedchambers. The contractor also built a new barn, 30 by 18 feet, with stalls for horses and cows.

In May 1771, while the house was being readied, Copley and Sukey departed by stagecoach for New York, leaving Copley's half brother, Henry Pelham, to direct the remodeling and attend to lawsuits in their absence. The trip was made in response to an offer by Captain Stephen Kemble, a British Army officer stationed on Manhattan Island, who guaranteed to find Copley a number of sitters there. So far as is known, Copley had never been out of Boston before. Although his reputation had outgrown its confines and brought him invitations from people in other colonial cities, he had always declined on the grounds that he was too busy. But Kemble's assurance that many of New York's most substantial citizens would sit for him, coupled with Copley's difficulties with the building operations on Beacon Hill, proved irresistible.

New York did not yet compare with Boston in size and commercial importance, but as headquarters for the British Army in North America, it was the gayest city in the colonies, with balls and banquets and an elegance of living beyond even that of New England's wealthiest families; for the less privileged there was ample enjoyment in the numerous taverns and bawdyhouses for which the city was notorious. Despite all the finery and frivolity Copley's loyalty was unswerving. "The city," he wrote Henry Pelham, "has more grand buildings than Boston, the streets much cleaner and some broader, but it is not Boston in my opinion yet."

Copley had notified Kemble in advance concerning the prices he expected to realize for his portraits: "the price of whole lengths 40 Guineas, half length 20, ¼ pieces or Busts, 10. Weither Men or Weomen makes

Mount Pleasant, Copley's estate on Boston's Beacon Hill, occupies the left background in this engraving of a 1768 watercolor by Christian Remick. The view, across Boston Common, reveals the rural setting of what is now the center of the city. After his marriage Copley had the middle of the three buildings on his property remodeled and took up residence there in 1772. Among his neighbors was John Hancock, whose tree-lined estate is seen to the right.

no differenc[e] in the pric[e] nor does the Dress, but Children in the ¼ peaces will be more, because of the addition of hands, which there must be when a Child is put in that size; but should the hands be omitted . . . the price will be the same as for a Mans or Womans without hands." Copley was putting a high value on his services out of town; at the time he seems to have been charging his fellow Bostonians less—between 11 and 15 guineas for oil portraits, depending upon size and, one suspects, the sitter's wealth. But he gauged his new market well. New York had no painter of comparable skill. Although nameless limners had plied a brisk trade among the Dutch of Nieuw Amsterdam and the Hudson Valley in the 17th and early 18th Centuries, this practice had died out, and nothing more sophisticated than the limner style had taken its place. About the only painter of any note in New York in Copley's time was John Durand, who had first arrived in Manhattan around 1766, possibly from France. Durand had painted some marvelously winsome and entertaining portraits (*page 104*) in a stiff, quasi-folk manner, but had left for Virginia the year before Copley's arrival.

As it turned out, Copley had to lengthen his stay in New York from an intended three months to seven. He was so busy, he wrote his half brother, that "I hardly get time to eat my victuals." The many letters he sent Henry somewhat dispute this claim. They indicate that he found a great deal of time to receive "vast numbers of people of the first Rank," to dine out with Sukey and to prowl New York; one letter discourses on the price of pineapples in Manhattan as compared with Boston. He also worried a lot about the progress at the Beacon Hill estate and sent Henry some fruit and laurel trees and "butiful" flowering bushes to plant there. Nevertheless, Copley did turn out a prodigious quantity of work: no fewer than 37 bust-length portraits in oils and several paintings of children. According to the price schedule he had quoted to Captain Kemble, he thus earned at least 370 guineas in seven months—as much as, if not more than, he would have earned at home in a year.

Many of the New York paintings have disappeared. Most of Copley's sitters there were loyalists who fled to England with all their household goods, portraits included, at the outbreak of the Revolution in 1775. Some of Copley's pictures may have been destroyed, while others may even now be masquerading as the work of other artists. For a long time this fate befell Copley's likeness of Mrs. Thomas Gage, the beautiful American-born wife of the general who commanded all British forces in the colonies until shortly after hostilities erupted. Convinced that it was "beyond Compare the best Ladys portrait I ever drew," Copley sent it to London for the 1772 exhibition of the recently founded Royal Academy, his first picture to be publicly shown in England since *Young Lady with a Bird and Dog* five years earlier. The painting hangs in the Gage family home in Sussex to this day, but for generations it was attributed to an English artist, Nathaniel Dance, and its sitter was thought to have been Mrs. Gage's daughter. Only in the last decade or so has the portrait been restored to its rightful creator and subject.

Those productions of Copley's New York sojourn that survive and are identifiable show further changes in his style. Their colors tend to be more restrained than in most of Copley's previous works; there is greater reliance on modeling in dark and light, with the gradations handled more subtly. A number of the New York oils are as simply composed as Copley's pastels, starkly devoid of accessories or architectural setting. The heads of the New York sitters are placed lower on the canvas than had been Copley's habit, and are thus set off with a depth of space above and around them that strengthens the reality of the portraiture.

At one point during his busy New York stay Copley found time for a two-week side trip to Philadelphia. What it lacked in gaiety the city made up by its absorption in cultural matters. A number of its leading citizens, like William Allen, the Chief Justice of Pennsylvania, were art enthusiasts and collectors; it was Allen who had contributed part of the money that enabled the young Pennsylvanian Benjamin West to go to Italy for further art study in 1760, the first step in his spectacular success abroad. The purpose of Copley's visit to Philadelphia was in fact to see Allen's collection, with its excellent copies of paintings by Titian and Correggio. A copy of Titian's *Venus* especially delighted Copley. He wrote Henry that he found it "fine in coloring, I think beyond any picture I have seen. . . . There is no minuteness in the finishing; everything is bold and easy."

Copley and his wife were back in Boston early in January of 1772. Perhaps buoyed by his venture, he soon undertook another: his one attempt at architectural design. In June a committee met to consider the rebuilding of the Brattle Square Church, and "the plan and Elevation of a Meeting House, with the Steple compleat, exhibited by Mr. Copley . . . was much admired for its Elegance and Grandure." However, the estimated cost of carrying out his ideas proved too great, and the career of John Singleton Copley, architect, ended abruptly at this point.

The rejection of his design could not have weighed too heavily on Copley, however, for that same year he was riding the very crest of his fame and prosperity as the leading portrait painter in the colonies. A young admirer who was destined to make his own mark on American painting,

John Trumbull, was taken to call on the artist at his Beacon Hill home. "We found Mr. Copley dressed to receive a party of friends at dinner," Trumbull recalled in his autobiography. "I remember his dress and appearance—an elegant looking man, dressed in fine maroon cloth, with gold buttons—this dazzling to my unpracticed eye!—but his paintings, the first I had ever seen deserving the name, riveted, absorbed my attention, and renewed all my desires to enter upon such a pursuit."

Not all of Copley's admirers were so unconditionally impressed. One William Carson, a resident of the Rhode Island colony, wrote praising him for a portrait of Mrs. Carson but unabashedly offered some advice. "Strange objects strongly strike the senses, and violent passions affect the mind," Carson declared. "To gain reputation, you should paint something new, to catch the sight and fix the attention." He then suggested that Copley paint a heart-rending scene of a sick child in a cradle, surrounded by the mother, "her face and attitude expressing hope and fear," an officious but sympathizing nurse, a long-visaged doctor and a female friend who looks on in indifference. Such a picture, Carson assured Copley, "will gain you more money than all you can get by face painting in Seven years."

Copley did not, of course, act on Carson's well-meaning advice, nor could he have. The kind of sentimentalized anecdote Carson was suggesting was entirely out of keeping with the painter's realistic bent and his lofty concept of what constituted great art. Interestingly enough, however, had he heeded Carson in 1772 he would have anticipated a major American art trend of the 19th Century; just such scenes, and others depicting homely events of everyday life, would pervade American painting—and much of Europe's—throughout the Victorian era. Still, in a very different context from the one Carson intended, Copley would soon become aware that "violent passions" could affect the mind.

Early in 1772, not long after Copley painted the lovely wife of General Thomas Gage, the general wrote to a friend in England: "Profound tranquility reigns in America." In the light of what followed, the British commander in the colonies would seem to have been deluding himself, but the fact is that in the years immediately preceding the Revolution there were long periods of quiet when the colonists went about their business as usual. Until open hostilities broke out in 1775, the colonists regarded themselves as freeborn Englishmen and felt no need to cut loose from the mother country. As the eminent historian Samuel Eliot Morison says, "Americans did not start off . . . with the conviction that they were entitled to a separate and independent nation. They never felt . . . that they were so downtrodden by tyrannical masters as to make independence the only solution. On the contrary, Americans were not only content but proud to be part of the British imperium. But they did feel very strongly that they were entitled to all constitutional rights that Englishmen possessed in England." It was this belief in their rights, and in the need to defend them, that caused what disruptions there were in the tranquillity of pre-Revolutionary America.

Although some of the disruptions directly or indirectly involved Copley and his relatives, the artist's role in the troubled events that ultimately culminated in revolution has sometimes been exaggerated. Some writers have pictured him as a patriot, others as a staunch adherent of the Crown. Actually he was neither. Despite the fact that his sitters included both freedom-minded Whigs and loyalist Tories, and despite his marriage into a prominent Tory family, Copley kept aloof from any appearance of sympathy with either political faction. The true explanation may lie in a comment he once made in a letter to Benjamin West. Politics, he declared, was "neither pleasing to an artist or advantageous to the Art itself."

He could not, however, entirely escape the effects of the growing unrest around him. As far back as September 1765, when he wrote to Captain Bruce in London notifying him that *Boy with a Squirrel* was on its way, Copley mentioned the violence that had shattered the calm of Boston the month before as the result of the Stamp Act. This act, recently passed by Parliament without any attempt being made to consult the colonies, called for a tax to be levied on them to help pay the cost of maintaining a British army in America for their protection. The tax itself took the form of a stamp that had to be bought and affixed to all newspapers, almost every legal document, liquor and marriage licenses, appointments to office, school or college diplomas—even to playing cards, one of the colonists' favorite means of diversion. Any offense against the Stamp Act was to be tried before a British admiralty court, without benefit of trial by jury.

The colonies greeted the Stamp Act with loud cries of "taxation without representation!" When the stamps first appeared in Boston in August 1765, popular indignation turned to fury; there were riots, arson and the hanging in effigy of those responsible for the Act and its enforcement. Enforcement indeed proved impossible, since few colonists would buy the detested stamps. Soon Parliament repealed the Act and tranquillity reigned again until the Townshend Act of 1767. This was an effort to collect taxes in the colonies without going to the extremes of the Stamp Act, by imposing duties on a few key imports such as glass, paper and tea. The Townshend Act, too, stirred resistance and also bloodshed, although some scholars argue that the bloodshed was in fact caused by the anger of Boston workingmen over some British soldiers who were moonlighting at a rope factory.

In any event, the British garrison in the city had had to be reinforced to keep order. Bostonians had long been irked at the presence of any British troops, since they had to help feed and quarter them. Sporadic clashes between Redcoats and citizens finally led to a confrontation on March 5, 1770. All that day belligerent mobs roamed the streets. Late in the afternoon a jeering crowd pelted a sentry near the Customs House with snowballs and other missiles, and a detachment of guards was called out to protect him. One Redcoat was felled by a stick or club, and the inevitable happened: the soldiers fired on the crowd. According to one account, three civilians were killed and two mortally wounded; other tallies list five killed and six wounded. Ironically, this occurred on the very day that Parliament repealed all the duties imposed by the Townshend Act except the tax on tea.

The Boston Massacre, as it is called, roused anger throughout the col-

This seal is the infamous "stamp" that the British Parliament in 1765 ordered affixed to, or embossed on, all American legal documents and such diverse objects as newspapers, diplomas and boxes of playing cards. The colonials bitterly objected, not so much to the price of the stamp (which varied from four pence to 20 shillings), but to the fact that Parliament had acted without consulting them. As a result, the stamp appeared on few American documents; colonial resentment forced repeal of the Stamp Act just one year after its passage.

onies, and in Boston inspired the most politically inflammatory work of art ever produced in America. This was an engraving of the event published on March 26, 1770, and titled *The Bloody Massacre Perpetrated in King Street Boston on March 5, 1770, by a party of the 29th Regt*. The artist was Paul Revere, who is less well known to history as a printmaker than as a master silversmith and Revolutionary firebrand.

As it happened, the circulation of prints of Revere's work gave Copley an intimate glimpse of the trigger temper of his times. Revere's engraving is an almost exact duplicate of an engraving of the massacre that Copley's half brother claimed to have done earlier. Pelham, then 21, had apparently been experimenting with the tools of his father's trade, and a bitter letter from him to Revere on March 29 indicates that he had some time previously sent Revere a proof of his own engraving, possibly for his advice. "When I heard that you was cutting a plate of the late Murder," Pelham wrote, "I thought it impossible, as I knew you was not capable of doing it unless you copied it from mine . . . I thought I had entrusted it in the hands of a person who had more regard to the dictates of Honour and Justice." Pelham added that he considered himself robbed "as truly as if you had plundered me on the highway."

Whether he was justified in his charge of plagiarism cannot be proved. In any case he went ahead and published his nearly identical version of the Boston Massacre two weeks after Paul Revere's. There is but one striking difference between the two engravings, and it appears in the accompanying captions. Although both listed the same five men killed and six wounded, Pelham also quoted from the Bible, deploring the bloodshed and the disregard for God shown by the British in shooting down His people. Revere's caption is much more violent. Where Pelham had his Biblical reproof, Revere had some verses, possibly his own, which included the following:

> Unhappy Boston! See thy Sons deplore,
> Thy hallow'd Walks besmeared with guiltless Gore
> While faithless P--n and his savage bands
> With murderous rancour stretch their bloody Hands,
> Like fierce Barbarians grinning o'er their Prey,
> Approve the Carnage, and enjoy the Day.

("Faithless P--n" was Captain Thomas Preston, commander of the guard at the Customs House.)

Pelham's engraving proved less effective than Revere's. With its incendiary caption, Revere's work was reprinted again and again and in many different forms, and eventually proved a major factor in consolidating the anti-British sentiment that led to the Revolution. Its influence did not end even with that struggle. It was reissued well into the 19th Century, and in the decade before the Civil War a new version of it provided a propaganda tool for those who favored the abolition of slavery. Although neither Pelham nor Revere had pictured him so, one of the victims of the Boston Massacre was a black man, Crispus Attucks, and the abolitionists seized upon him as an early black martyr in American history. A print that appeared in 1854 made the dying Attucks the central figure,

The Bloody Massacre perpetrated in King—Street BOSTON on March 5th 1770 by a party of the 29th REGT

Engrav'd Printed & Sold by Paul Revere Boston

Unhappy Boston! see thy Sons deplore, / Thy hallow'd Walks besmear'd with guiltless Gore. / While faithless P——n and his savage Bands, / With murd'rous Rancour stretch their bloody Hands; / Like fierce Barbarians grinning o'er their Prey, / Approve the Carnage, and enjoy the Day.

If scalding drops from Rage from Anguish Wrung / If speechless Sorrows lab'ring for a Tongue, / Or if a weeping World can ought appease / The plaintive Ghosts of Victims such as these; / The Patriot's copious Tears for each are shed, / A glorious Tribute which embalms the Dead.

But know Fate summons to that awful Goal, / Where Justice strips the Murd'rer of his Soul: / Should venal C——ts the scandal of the Land, / Snatch the relentless Villain from her Hand, / Keen Execrations on this Plate inscrib'd, / Shall reach a Judge who never can be brib'd.

The unhappy Sufferers were Mess.rs Sam.l Gray, Sam.l Maverick, Jam.s Caldwell, Crispus Attucks & Pat.k Carr Killed. Six wounded; two of them (Christr Monk & John Clark) Mortally

Paul Revere's controversial engraving of the Boston Massacre *(left)*, which Copley's half brother, Henry Pelham, claimed was plagiarized from his own version *(below)*, is the more famous of the two, but by no means the better executed. Pelham's figures are more skillfully drawn, and the perspective of his buildings is more expert. Revere's print, however, was more biting and accusatory in tone, from the excoriating verse beneath the picture to the sign on the building at right—Butcher's Hall.

---

totally dominating the composition. Few propaganda pictures have endured so long or served two such different wars as Paul Revere's *Bloody Massacre Perpetrated in King Street Boston.*

Even with the aid of his inflammatory creation, Revere and like-minded friends had a hard time stoking the fires of anti-British feeling. Just as after the repeal of the Stamp Act, political calm returned after the Massacre and the withdrawal of most of the Townshend duties. Rising prosperity helped cool tempers: ship clearances in Boston's harbor doubled in number and the value of goods handled through New England ports quadrupled. The rhetoric of Revolutionists like Revere seemed to fall on deaf ears. It was during this more placid period that Copley painted some of the most prominent Revolutionary leaders.

His now-celebrated likeness of Paul Revere, however, probably was painted before Pelham's angry letter; very likely Copley would have found it embarrassing to confront Revere in the wake of his half brother's denunciation. The painting *(page 84)* shows Revere not in his capacity as political agitator but as a prime craftsman at his worktable; he is in his shirt sleeves and holds in his left hand one of his own exquisitely wrought silver teapots. The teapot, with Revere's fingers reflected in its rounded surface, may well be the most realistically painted piece of still life in all of Copley's portraits. Copley's rendition is no less convincing than the tea-

Silversmith Paul Revere created the elegant bowl above in 1768 as a salute to 92 members of the Massachusetts House of Representatives who courageously supported a boycott of English goods in protest against oppressive taxation. Its shape became so popular that it is now known as the "Revere bowl." Below is the graceful Revere teapot, thought to be pictured by Copley in his portrait of the craftsman at his worktable (*page 84*).

pot itself, which is preserved today in a glass case beneath Revere's portrait at the Museum of Fine Arts in Boston.

Another outspoken critic of the British whom Copley portrayed was Samuel Adams, one of the few intellectuals in the colonies who had consistently and persistently agitated against British rule. Adams based his opposition on the theory that the colonies had the right to be largely autonomous by virtue of their original charters. He thus fought every kind of rule imposed by the Crown and Parliament, whether taxes, legal or legislative controls, or military supervision.

In painting Adams, Copley posed him in a way that dramatically points up the man's fiery nature and unshakable beliefs. Short, stubby, his expression fiercely denunciatory, Adams stands behind a table and points with one hand to a document that symbolizes his political philosophy; its huge seal bears the words "Charter of William and Mary to Massachusetts." In his other hand he holds a scroll inscribed "Instructions of the Town of Boston." The picture shows Adams on the day after the Boston Massacre when, as a representative of the people, he confronted Thomas Hutchinson, Royal Lieutenant Governor of Massachusetts. "It was then, if fancy deceived me not, I saw his knees to tremble," Adams later wrote. "I thought I saw his face grow pale (and I enjoyed the sight) at the appearance of the determined citizens peremptorily demanding the redress of grievances."

Copley's portrait of Adams is believed to have been painted for his friend and fellow advocate of resistance, John Hancock, and it hung in Hancock's house next to Copley's on Beacon Hill. Copley also did two portraits of Hancock himself around the same time (*page 83*). Apparently neither he nor his patrons saw any conflict in memorializing the features of ardent Whigs while pursuing his normal contacts with loyalist Tories. But toward the end of 1772 a series of events began that gradually divided Whig and Tory beyond all hope of reconciliation. One of the most stirring of these events—the Boston Tea Party—profoundly and personally influenced Copley's future.

The prelude to all the trouble was the burning in March of 1772 of a British revenue cutter, the *Gaspé,* by Rhode Islanders. While hunting down New England merchant vessels thought to be engaged in smuggling, the *Gaspé* ran aground in Narragansett Bay. The commander was wounded, the crew was roughed up, and the ship itself was then set afire. Later in the year a board of inquiry arrived from London to investigate the affair. The people of Rhode Island proved closemouthed and the board failed to ferret out the culprits. But the very establishment of such a board seemed to the Rhode Islanders to violate their right to conduct their own legal affairs. By implication, it threatened the legal system of every other colony as well, and it caused a furor all along America's Atlantic seaboard.

Then London heaped fuel on the fire by deciding to pay the judges of the Massachusetts superior court from customs revenues—Crown funds —rather than through local taxation. Adams, Revere and their followers saw this as an effort to transform the colonial judiciary into a tool of the Crown, and formed a Committee of Correspondence in Boston to protest. Soon there were Committees of Correspondence everywhere, condemning not only London's meddling in judicial matters but other Parliamentary moves that were seen as curtailing colonial liberties.

The move that directly embroiled Copley concerned that innocent beverage, tea. Americans seem to have drunk more of it in the 1770s than they do coffee today. Millions of pounds of tea came into the colonies each year. Much of it came legally, on payment of the one tax remaining from the Townshend Act. But a great deal was also smuggled in and sold by colonial merchants at relatively low prices. Up to 1773 the British East India Company, which enjoyed a monopoly on transporting tea from the Orient, was compelled by law to sell it first to dealers in England, who paid a tax on it and transshipped it to America, where it was taxed a second time under the Townshend Act. In 1773 the East India Company prevailed upon Parliament to pass the Tea Act, permitting the shipment of tea direct to colonial ports; thereby the cost of transshipment, the middleman's profit and the English tax were eliminated. The Company now had only the Townshend Act duty to pay and could put down tea on American wharves at a price lower than that asked for the smuggled product. But merchants in the colonies discovered a catch: the Company would sell its tea only to a small, hand-picked group of American wholesalers, all loyalists. In Boston there were only five such dealers. One was Richard Clarke, Copley's father-in-law.

Whig merchants in Boston, excluded by this one-sided deal, protested furiously. An indignant broadside listing their grievances against the Company's agents brought a countering announcement from the agents that "we are resolved to buy and sell when and where we please; herein hop-

Shortly before open war broke out with England, Paul Revere published this satirical cartoon in a Boston magazine. He based some of its details on an English engraving, retaining the original figures of George III, seated at right, and his prime minister, Lord North, who faces him. Other figures are of Revere's own invention. At the far left, a symbolic America pleads for divine intercession, while at the right Cabinet ministers assure the King that all is well. But the hated Lord North is shown handing George a document abolishing civil and religious liberty in the colonies, and saying "This will quell the rebels." To indicate the King's empty-headedness, Revere depicted him with absolutely nothing to say.

ing for the Protection of Good Government: then let the Bellowing PA-TRIOT [the Whig merchants] throw out his thundering Bulls, they will only serve to soothe our sleep."

The forces represented by the Bellowing PATRIOT, however, were thundering about more than just the monopoly enjoyed by Copley's father-in-law and his fellow agents. Adams and other Whig leaders not only feared the threat to free enterprise but detected in the retention of the Townshend tea duty a Crown plot to sustain its right to tax the colonies. There was only one way to fight such tyranny, they argued: prevent the East India Company tea from being unloaded.

The matter came to a climax when three of the Company's tea ships sailed into Boston's harbor in November and December of 1773. At meetings conducted by the chief opponents of the tea tax, resolutions were drawn up demanding that the tea be returned to England. The resolutions were delivered to Copley's father-in-law and the Company's other consignees, but Governor Thomas Hutchinson ruled that the tea could not be shipped back, on the grounds that he had no instructions from London to do so.

The tension that gripped Boston at the time was vividly described by Henry Pelham in a letter to England. "The various and discordant Noises with which my Ears are continually assailed in the day, passing of Carts and a constant throng of People, the shouting of an undisciplined Rabble, the ringing of bells and sounding of Horns in the night when it might be expected that an universal silence should reign but instead of that nothing but a confused medley of the ratlings of Carriages, the noises of drums, and the infernal yell of those who are fighting for the possessions of the Devill. Last Tuesday Morng. a considerable number of Printed papers was pasted up, directed to the freemen of the Province inviting them to meet at Liberty Tree at 12 oClock the next day to receive the resignation upon Oath of those Gentle'n to whom the India Company have consigned their tea of the Commission and their promise of re-shiping it by the first opertunity. . . . The next morning incendiary letters were sent . . . to these genln . . . commanding upon their Perril their attendance."

Richard Clarke and the other loyalist tea agents did not show up as ordered and a mob tried to storm Clarke's warehouse. Their personal safety threatened, Clarke, his two sons, and the other agents and their families then took refuge in Castle William, a fort located on Castle Island in Boston's harbor and garrisoned by British soldiers. Protest assemblies continued to meet in the city. Plainly some go-between, a man respected by both sides but politically involved with neither, had to be found if any settlement was to be made. The man chosen was John Singleton Copley, eminently qualified by his friendship with the loyalists and his studio sessions with Adams and other key dissidents. To be sure, Copley was married to Clarke's daughter, but he had no connection with Clarke's business interests.

As a mediator seeking a peaceful solution to an explosive situation, Copley met alternately with the Whig leaders in Boston and the East India Company agents at Castle William. Both parties refused to compromise, and on December 1, 1773, the artist sent a message to one of his beleaguered brothers-in-law. At a town meeting, he reported, he had "made use of every argument my thoughts could suggest to draw the people from their unfavourable opinion of you, and to convince them your opposition was neither the effect of obstinacy or unfriendliness to the community; but altogether from necessity on your part to discharge a trust commited to you, a failure in which would subject you to ruin in your reputation as Merchants." Although Copley did not succeed in persuading his fellow townsmen to ease their demands, his arguments seem to have had some cooling effect on the Whig leaders, for he added that "I have been told and I believe it is true, that after I left the Meeting Addams said they must not expect you should Ruin your selves. I think all stands well at present."

Copley's efforts, however, proved futile. On December 16, 1773, a party of Revolutionists held the history-making Boston Tea Party. Dressed as Mohawk Indian warriors, they boarded the tea ships in the harbor and tossed 340 chests of tea into the water.

The Clarkes stayed on at Castle William. Late in the following April, Copley reported to them by letter that a mob had gathered outside his Beacon Hill house the previous night, demanding that he turn over to them his friend Colonel George Watson, a well-known loyalist who was shortly to be sworn in as a member of the governing Royal Council of Massachusetts. Watson had been at Copley's in the afternoon and had left, and the artist was able to convince the crowd of this. He ended his letter: "What if Mr. Watson had stayed, (as I pressed him to) to spend the night. I must either have given up a friend to the insult of a Mob or had my house pulled down and perhaps my family murthered."

For Copley, this spelled the end of his life in Boston. He had never entirely turned his eyes from Europe, and the Watson incident apparently decided him. With the political situation so inflammatory and the economic outlook so shaky, he saw no future for himself, at least for a good while, in Boston. Armed with letters of introduction to friends abroad from people in Boston, Philadelphia and other colonial cities, Copley sailed for England on June 10, 1774. He intended to visit London briefly and then proceed to Italy, the great fountainhead of art. Following Benjamin West's advice, he left his wife and children behind; West feared that Mrs. Copley's presence might involve her husband in a social whirl distracting to his pursuit of Europe's "higher Exalances in Art." Copley clearly intended, as soon as the troubles were over, to return to his house on Beacon Hill and to his flourishing practice as America's leading portrait painter. But the simmering hostility between the colonies and the mother country soon erupted into a long and bloody war of independence. And so he never came back.

By the time Copley sailed away from his native shores, he had painted some 350 portraits, of which 312 are known to exist today. He also left a tradition which other artists in America were to maintain and develop in their own ways. Just as Copley looked to England as the source and sanction of everything good in portrait painting, so a younger generation of Americans looked to Boston and to Copley.

In the dozen years before he left America in 1774, Copley reached his peak of productivity and achievement as a portraitist. He not only mastered the technique of creating accurate likenesses but became expert at rendering the signs of material success—rich fabrics, gleaming furniture—that his sitters demanded. With few precedents to guide him, Copley acquired ever more skill at rounding his figures. If their poses seem a bit stiff to modern eyes, his subjects nevertheless dominate the canvas and project a living presence.

With the departure of his most serious rival, Joseph Blackburn, business boomed for Copley; he found his services booked solid for as long as a year in advance. Prosperity and increased social status were his rewards, but for all this Copley felt frustrated. Portraiture was too limited a means of expression. He longed to try his hand at religious or historical scenes, ambitious pictures of the sort favored by the European artists he admired. The fulfillment of this dream awaited him in England, but meanwhile he prudently pursued his gift for portraiture, and in so doing compiled a matchless record of the small but influential upper class of colonial America. Its men and women were provincial rather than sophisticated, money-conscious and self-esteeming, yet straightforward and stalwart. Their affectations could not hide their essential vigor, and it was this quality, above all others, that Copley so tellingly memorialized.

Colonial Faces

Mrs. Thomas Boylston, 1766

Mrs. Thomas Boylston of Boston, mother of eight and a grandmother many times over, fixed a benign gaze on Copley as he worked at her portrait. Although she was 70 at the time, her complexion retains some of its bloom —Copley took great pains to capture his sitters' skin tones exactly—and her hair is ungrayed. Her lustrous satin dress is testimony to the comfortable way of life afforded by her husband's wealth as a food supplier.

YALE UNIVERSITY ART GALLERY, NEW HAVEN, BEQUEST OF EDITH MALVINA K. WETMORE

Mary Toppan (Mrs. Benjamin Pickman), 1763

Mrs. Benjamin Pickman was 19 and had been married a year when Copley painted her, self-assured and plump-faced (the halolike effect around her head indicates changes he made to increase the illusion of roundness).

The Pickmans were Tories who went to England when the Revolution broke out. But after the war they returned to Massachusetts where, despite their earlier loyalties, Pickman became treasurer of the town of Salem.

Mary Turner Sargent, 1763

Wearing a green version of the same dress as Mrs. Pickman's, Mrs. Daniel Sargent emerges as ethereally elegant. The duplication of costume may have come about because Copley's sitters sometimes chose their outfits from prints of portraits of stylish Europeans. In later years Mrs. Sargent recalled that at one of her 15 or 16 sittings with Copley, when he left the room she had peeked at the canvas only to find it "all rubbed out."

Mrs. Ezekiel Goldthwait, 1771

The warm, hospitable personality of Mrs. Ezekiel Goldthwait comes through strongly across the centuries. She was a noted hostess: one "genteel dinner" at her home, accompanied by an "incomparable Madeira," was appreciatively recorded by a guest, John Adams. She was also a talented gardener, and presumably the firm, ripe fruit she proffers—painted with brushstrokes smoothed almost to invisibility *(detail left)*—is home-grown.

Nathaniel Sparhawk, 1764

John Hancock, 1765

Genial in his flowing wig, Nathaniel Sparhawk belonged to a family that had been in America four generations. Sparhawks tended to be clergymen or public servants, and Nathaniel was a judge—with a reputation for furthering his relatives' interests while on the bench. This was Copley's first large full-length portrait; his inexperience led him to overdo the architectural setting by which he tried to symbolize his subject's status.

The year before Copley painted him, 28-year-old John Hancock had inherited a fortune and a thriving shipping business. Here he sits at an imposing ledger, tensely aware of his new executive responsibilities. Radical politically, Hancock helped finance the Revolution. But he could be remiss in lesser money matters: Copley's half brother, trying to present the painter's bill, repeatedly found the tycoon indisposed with "violent headack."

MUSEUM OF FINE ARTS, BOSTON, GIFT OF JOSEPH W., WILLIAM B. AND EDWARD H. R. REVERE

Paul Revere, 1768-1770

Skilled craftsman and soon to be Revolutionary hero, Paul Revere holds a silver teapot he has made on his leather hammering pillow, as if pondering a projected design before he takes up an engraving tool. Stocky and dark—his father was French—he wears no wig and has left his hair unpowdered. Revere, an activist rather than an intellectual, amassed much wealth but, as an obituary noted, put it "always at the service of indigent worth."

Nicholas, the eldest son of Mrs. Boylston (*page 76*), was a quiet man who, like his father, became a successful merchant. Perhaps because of an early devotion to business, he did not attend Harvard, as most moneyed young Bostonians did, but he endowed the college generously. Unlike his Tory parents, he supported American independence. Here he wears a fashionable at-home costume: satin turban and damask dressing gown.

84

Nicholas Boylston, 1767

Daniel Crommelin Verplanck, 1771

On a foray away from Boston Copley produced this portrait of nine-year-old Daniel Verplanck, a banker's son and scion of an old Dutch family of New York. The boy sits on the steps of the family mansion, his round head

neatly cropped, his pose carefully held, his glance shy. The detail at right shows Copley's skill at conveying texture: the squirrel's bushy tail, Daniel's flesh and clothes, and the metal chain are all rendered with total fidelity.

IV

Patriots
and Painters

In the long winter months following Copley's failure to mediate the affair of the Boston Tea Party, the spark of rebellion smoldered and grew. Those New Englanders who were neither diehard Tories nor ardent Whigs tried to see a peaceful way out of the dilemma. But throughout the spring and summer of 1774 the British authorities tightened their repressive measures. In retribution for the Tea Party and less blatant acts of sabotage and disobedience, they attempted to starve Boston into submission by cutting off supplies of food. On behalf of his city the fiery Paul Revere traveled to New York and Philadelphia to seek help, and returned home with pledges of assistance; the New Yorkers alone promised provisions enough to withstand a 10-year siege. Soon sheep, rice and wheat began flowing in to relieve the Bostonians, and a new spirit of determination and unity arose among them. Companies of militia were formed, arsenals were assembled, and observation posts were set up to watch the movement of British troops and ships.

By the time Copley left Boston for England in June of 1774, tensions were high but no overt conflict had yet erupted. On the fringes of the city occasional violence flared between Yankee citizen and British soldier, and the patriots succeeded in harassing the British garrison in a number of small ways. General Thomas Gage, the British commander, found that supplies for new barracks needed to house his growing army were destroyed or diverted, workmen were incited to stay off the job, and it was chill November before many of the troops could move into their quarters. One of the minor afflictions devised by the patriots for the Redcoats was a lethal brew called Kill Devil that local tavernkeepers served to the Britishers. A number of deaths were attributed to the concoction.

By the early spring of 1775 Gage had become increasingly apprehensive about the safety of his troops and the rumored activity of the patriots' militant organization, the Sons of Liberty. Events were leading inexorably to that memorable night in April when Paul Revere made his heroic ride. As every schoolboy knows, it was the evening of the 18th when two lamps hung in the belfry of Boston's Old North Church signaled that a party of British troops was being moved out of the city by sea in-

89

This engraving, one of a set of four by Amos Doolittle, is based on Ralph Earl's paintings of the Battles of Lexington and Concord, made not long after those skirmishes had taken place. Earl, a loyalist sympathizer, depicted a large contingent of British troops, some of whom are deploying for a house-to-house search of Concord. Meanwhile, two of their officers, Colonel Smith (*left*) and Major Pitcairn (*right*), reconnoiter the countryside from a hillside cemetery overlooking the town.

stead of by land. Spy reports had already confirmed the troops' destination, and Revere galloped off to rouse the militant leaders, Samuel Adams and John Hancock, from their hide-out at Lexington, and to warn other Sons of Liberty guarding a powder arsenal at Concord. Revere alerted Adams and Hancock just in time, for the following morning, shortly after they fled, Gage's 500 soldiers marched onto Lexington green with muskets loaded.

No one knows who fired the fateful first shot "heard 'round the world," but before the smoke had cleared, eight Americans lay dead on the green and 10 were wounded. Still, no actual confrontation took place; just before the deadly volley the colonials had been ordered by their commander to disperse. As they withdrew, the Redcoats re-formed and marched on Concord to root out a cache of military stores. It was at the bridge north of Concord that a second historic skirmish occurred, this time between a detachment of the British soldiers and the Yankee Minutemen gathered from all over the countryside. Fearful that the British were bent on razing the town, the Americans attacked at the bridge. A resounding volley sent the nervous Redcoats scrambling, and thus began a long and costly retreat back to safety under the guns of British ships lying in Boston's harbor. The Minutemen, firing from the shelter of stone fences and from behind trees, dogged the confused and frustrated foe all the way. By nightfall, the British had incurred 275 casualties in dead, wounded and missing. The rebels—for now the provincials were truly a people in revolt—tallied only 93 losses.

Within two months full-fledged war had broken out between the colonies and the mother country. On Saturday, June 17, a year and a day after Copley had left his native city, a battle took place for possession of a strategic height overlooking Boston's harbor. Not merely hundreds, but several thousand men saw action in the Battle of Bunker's Hill. Before the British gained the hill, more than 1,000 of their troops lost their lives. Some 140 Americans died; among them was Major General Joseph Warren, the Boston physician whose portrait Copley had painted 10 years earlier.

The bloodshed, and the losses of men both distinguished and nameless, were to continue for almost 10 more years. In 1783, after the British surrender at Yorktown, a treaty of peace was concluded between England and the proud new United States of America, and the American Congress sent its first Ambassador to London. Copley, long since established in his English career, took special pleasure in painting the portraits of two old Whig friends, John Adams and his beloved wife Abigail, who arrived to occupy the new American Embassy, but with a fine touch of even-handedness he also painted those staunch defenders of the Crown, Admiral Richard Howe and Charles Lord Cornwallis.

How Copley would have fared had he stayed in Boston can only be surmised. It is possible that in his departure his native land lost a potential freedom fighter, for his basic approval of the cause of American independence—and his opportunistic eye for the winning side—may ultimately have led him to throw in his lot with the rebels. What is more certain is that in his leaving, America lost its greatest artist. To be sure, during the war there was little market for an artist's services, except for the execution of such patriotic and satirical engravings as Paul Revere turned out to rally public sentiment. But other artists who might have learned from Copley were deprived of his counsel.

Some who rose to prominence during and after the war years—Charles Willson Peale, John Trumbull and Gilbert Stuart among them—traveled to Europe to make up for the lack of local inspiration. But they eventually returned home to become the mainstays of the 19th Century tradition of portraiture and historical painting. Other men, perhaps less talented and ambitious—and decidedly less well known—continued to paint in the colonial manner. With rare exceptions, none of these painters left the country, and most remained at work in their native regions. Essentially self-taught, they followed very much in the tradition of the pre-Copley limners and, like these anonymous predecessors, they are now widely characterized as folk, or primitive, artists. But whatever weaknesses of technique and artistic vision they may have had, they are neither anonymous nor primitive.

One of these painters is closely linked with Revolutionary history. Ralph Earl was born in Massachusetts in 1751 into a family of farmers and craftsmen originally from Rhode Island. Possibly he had some instruction in art from a teacher in Newport, although no proof exists. In any case, when he was 24 Earl set himself up in a studio in New Haven, near Yale College. In the summer after the skirmishes at Lexington and Concord he and a young engraver with whom he had become friendly, Amos Doolittle, decided to make some capital out of these already historic encounters by visiting the scenes of the action with a view to depicting the events that had taken place there. Earl was to paint the pictures, and Doolittle was then to engrave them for a large print edition to be sold at six shillings a set, eight shillings for a watercolor-tinted version. The collaboration was a cordial one from the first: Doolittle's account of their trip recalls that he was required to pose in various soldierly attitudes—loading a gun, crouching behind a stone wall—while Earl sketched.

Back in New Haven, Earl produced four imaginative paintings of the battles at Lexington and Concord and Doolittle then based four engravings on them. Several complete sets of the engravings still exist, although they are very rare, and one of Earl's original oils survives, the oldest known painting of a historic event to be produced in America. Second only to a few of Paul Revere's engravings and to Henry Pelham's rendition of the 1770 Boston Massacre, Earl's painting and Doolittle's prints are vital documents in the history of the republic—if not in the history of art. They are rather crude and amateurish; perspective is distorted, figures are drawn in childlike, stick fashion, and the landscape itself is as nondescript as if the two artists had never seen the actual sites. Moreover, both the painting and the engravings seem strongly slanted in favor of the British: it is they who predominate in the scenes.

In the case of Earl, at least, there is an explanation for this choice of emphasis. Although he was a native New Englander, and although his own father served as a captain in the Revolutionary army, Earl was a confirmed Tory. Unlike the middle-of-the-road Copley, he stood squarely on the side of the British, and his staunch beliefs cost him dearly among his countrymen. Several times he was called before Revolutionary tribunals and once was forced to leave Connecticut on pain of imprisonment. Except for his father's rank, he might have been executed for consorting with the enemy, for on at least one occasion he helped to get a message to the British command that saved some of their troops from a rebel ambush. Things finally got so hot for him that he was forced to quit the country. Earl set sail for England in 1778, eluding the patriots by posing as a servant to the departing British quartermaster general.

Shortly before that, however, Earl's artistic inclination led him to do something totally out of line with his politics. He painted a portrait of Roger Sherman of Connecticut *(page 88)*, the least likely man a passionate Tory would want to do business with. Once described by John Adams as "an Old Puritan, as honest as an angel and as firm in the cause of American Independence as Mount Atlas," Sherman was a fascinating character and a prime early example of the self-made man. Massachusetts-born, he learned the cobbler's trade from his father, and meanwhile augmented a desultory common-school education by wide readings in the classics, mathematics and law. After his father died, he joined his brother in the Connecticut town of New Milford, reportedly walking the 100-odd miles from Massachusetts with his cobbler's bench on his back. Within a few years he was made county surveyor and, as a result of his opportunities in this capacity, became a large landowner. He also served as town clerk, a deacon of the church, a school committeeman and the owner of the town's first store. Capping these early accomplishments, Sherman wrote a treatise on Connecticut economics and a series of al-

This portrait of the third Chief Justice of the United States, Oliver Ellsworth, and his wife reveals the sophistication the artist, Ralph Earl, had acquired in seven years in England. Compared with Earl's portrait of Roger Sherman *(page 88)*, the figures of the Ellsworths are much more expertly handled. The painting also includes a trademark of Earl's later work—landscapes that tell something about the sitters. In this painting, set in Ellsworth's library, the exterior of the home is seen through the window.

manacs based on his own mathematical and astronomical computations. Still later he became a lawyer, a justice of the peace, a judge of the county court, a member of the Connecticut General Assembly—all before he was 40—and ultimately a signer of the Declaration of Independence and one of the framers of the Constitution.

Earl's portrait of Sherman has the quality of a strong mask. The eyes are deep-set and penetrating; the expression is austere. The full-length figure sits in a Windsor chair, a Connecticut product; the chair is rather more expertly handled than the figure. In its meticulous rendering, as well as in Sherman's pose, Earl seems to have taken a leaf from Copley, but there is none of the charm and gloss of Copley's portraits. Instead, this earliest known portrait by Earl is powerful and somber, an altogether striking work.

Earl spent most of his time during his seven years in England in the East Anglian county of Norfolk, painting portraits that were flattering to his sitters, but scarcely up to the works of the more accomplished painters in London. In time, Earl improved his draftsmanship and moved to the big city to pit his talents against the field. He seems to have gotten some help from Benjamin West, and he also met Copley. Then, in 1785, he returned to America.

With the war's end Earl's previous Tory sympathies no longer counted against him. Lacking an artistic reputation in his own country, he disarmed his compatriots with claims of distinction abroad. He made one in an advertisement in a New York newspaper: "Last Sunday arrived in town from England, by way of Boston, Mr. Ralph Earl, a native of Massachusetts; he has passed a number of years in London under those distinguished and most celebrated Masters in Painting, Sir Joshua Reynolds, Mr. West and Mr. Copley." The notice drew attention, and commissions began to come Earl's way. But his hard drinking and free-spending habits caught up with him, and soon he was in a New York jail for debt. An up-and-coming young lawyer, Alexander Hamilton, soon to be President Washington's Secretary of the Treasury, came to Earl's rescue, commissioning a portrait of Mrs. Hamilton. The lady, showing remarkable poise, posed for Earl in his prison. Perhaps amused by this novelty, several of Hamilton's influential friends also sat for the painter behind the stone walls. Despite this curious interlude, however, Earl's credit in New York was overdrawn. He spent the rest of his career back in Connecticut, traveling from town to village making portraits of provincial gentry and doing an occasional landscape.

Winthrop Chandler's study of the Reverend Ebenezer Devotion seated in his library is a knowledgeable and convincing portrayal of a fascinating man. The clergyman's books, which Chandler took great pains to depict, show an unusual range of interests. Among the works are treatises by the liberal 17th Century English philosopher John Locke, several volumes of the London journal *The Spectator*, Watt's *Sermons*, Rapin's *History of England* and Sir Isaac Newton's *Opticks*.

Another post-Copley painter, Winthrop Chandler, remained more constant to Connecticut. He was born there in 1747, on a large farm in Windham County straddling a rise known as Chandler Hill, and died there in 1790. So far as is known his excursions elsewhere were limited to neighboring Massachusetts. He is believed to have spent part of his youth in Boston, as an apprentice to an artisan-painter, possibly a family acquaintance, John Gore, who was also the father of the children Copley had painted so charmingly *(pages 28-29)*. Gore owned a shop, the Sign of the Painter's Arms, where he not only sold all kinds of art supplies from gold leaf to brushes and crayons, but offered "coach and carpet paint-

ing in the best and cheapest manner." The rather small circle of artisans in Boston at the time makes it likely that young Chandler would have known Copley and have seen some of his best American work. The way Chandler later posed his sitters, surrounding them with the appurtenances of their status, and the way he modeled faces are strongly reminiscent of the Bostonian's style.

The earliest known portraits by Chandler are those of the Reverend and Mrs. Ebenezer Devotion of Woodstock, Connecticut. The minister —the more interestingly portrayed of the two—is posed in the Copley manner, sitting at a table. But there is also something new. He is posed against a background of richly bound books on shelves, a library set forth in minute and intense detail. In devoting so much attention to the books, Chandler is not merely showing off his virtuosity. He is trying to tell us something, and what he is telling us is that the Reverend Dr. Ebenezer Devotion, whose name sounds like that of a caricatured religious hypocrite in a Sheridan play, was one of the more liberal ecclesiastics of his time. Many of the book titles are still legible in the painting; most are tracts upholding the more enlightened side of the religious controversies then raging. The doctrine of man's inherent sinfulness, along with all the rest of the sadistic horror that had attached itself to religion in colonial New England, was on the way out, and Ebenezer Devotion was apparently one of those responsible for the demise.

Chandler's portraits of his brother, Captain Samuel Chandler, and Samuel's wife are even closer to Copley than the Devotion portraits. In these likenesses, Devotion's wrinkled, parchmentlike look gives way to rounded plasticity, very much in Copley's style. The artist is somewhat awkward in articulating the figures and adjusting them to the space they occupy. But in his study of his brother, in particular, he reveals what was to become his most remarkable trait—his ability to individualize the features of the face. Samuel Chandler is very sharply characterized. Moreover, in sign of his service in the Revolutionary army, a marvelously detailed battle of Minutemen and Redcoats goes on outside the window by which he sits. His three-cornered hat rests on a polished table to his left, but is not reflected in its surface; such reflections require more subtlety of paintercraft than his brother could muster. But the artist makes a tentative

This charming landscape, with its perfect symmetry and crude animal figures —including a ghostly deer—was produced by an unknown Connecticut artist in about 1750. Painted on wood and almost six feet wide, it was originally mounted over the fireplace in a home in Woodbury. Landscapes were a favorite theme of overmantels, as well as of the wall paintings that itinerant artisans were often asked to do. Most of the murals have disappeared with the houses they decorated, but those painted on wooden panels and therefore portable, like this overmantel, exist as the oldest surviving landscape art in America.

pass at such a reflection in the companion portrait, *Mrs. Samuel Chandler.* Mrs. Chandler also sits at a polished table. She has a ribbon bow at each elbow, and the one nearer the table is muddily mirrored in it.

Mrs. Chandler is placed in an alcove full of books on shelves like those in *Dr. Ebenezer Devotion;* it would be more accurate to say she is squeezed into the alcove. But her costume—filmy organdy over brown silk; large violet ribbon bows on the sleeves, at the neck and on the cap; white lace cuffs; long lace mitts and flowered fan—is a miracle of descriptive realism that Copley might well have envied. Copley, for all the detail in his American works, shows us only what we might reasonably expect to see with a moment's contemplation. A folk artist like Chandler, however, does not contemplate, he catalogues. His images are accumulations of memory, not observations of fact. It is this, wholly aside from any question of technical excellence or crudity, that puts his work in an esthetic category all its own.

Chandler is the archetype of the primitive painter or sculptor whose foremost characteristic, as Robert Louis Stevenson once put it, is his "combination of the childish courage of the amateur, attempting all things, like the schoolboy upon his slate, with the manly perseverance of the artist, who does not know when he is conquered."

Despite his labors, Chandler had a hard time making a living at his art. Many of his paintings are family portraits for which presumably he got no fee. One of the most interesting of them, especially for the light it throws on one of the social and professional conventions of the time, is his likeness of his brother-in-law, Dr. William Glysson *(page 102).* Shown seated, with a gold-headed cane in his right hand, Dr. Glysson is taking the pulse of a lady patient who is decorously hidden behind curtains, with only her hand and wrist protruding. That Chandler's painting is a document of the medical practice of his day and not just a bow to the inhibitions of one shy Connecticut matron is borne out by other, similar portrayals of doctors of the period *(page 103).*

By the late 1780s Chandler was forced to support himself as a house painter in Worcester, Massachusetts. Ill and widowed, he had to sell off most of the Connecticut property he had inherited, and in one civic record of 1789 he was described as "Winthrop Chandler, poor, diseased, insolvent.'' When he died the following year, a local newspaper noted his passing in an obituary that can serve as a requiem for hundreds of early Americans whose talents found inadequate outlet, or no outlet at all: ''By profession he was a house painter, but many good likenesses on canvas shew he could guide the pencil of a limner. . . . The world was not his enemy, but as is too common, his genius was not nourished on the bosom of encouragement. Embarrassment, like strong weeds in a garden of delicate flowers, checked his usefulness and disheartened the man.''

But more than ''strong weeds'' was harvested from Chandler's art, for at least several other painters were inspired to imitate him. Most of them are anonymous, identifiable only through the stylistic similarities between their work and his. One artist, however, is somewhat better identified; indeed the details of his life history, although scant, seem to confirm a link with Chandler.

Reuben Moulthrop is one of those painters of 18th Century America who are so obscure that until recently many people who owned their works did not know who painted them. Moulthrop himself, whose ''discovery'' in the 1930s was largely the work of the art historian William Sawitzky and his wife, Susan, was especially ignored because in his own time he had a reputation not as a painter but as a showman. In partnership with various relatives and a man named Daniel Bowen, Moulthrop toured New England's towns and cities with an exhibition of waxwork figures he had sculpted. Unfortunately, none of these is known to have survived, probably because of their fragile medium. But Moulthrop also painted, and these works are preserved in considerable numbers.

A prime clue in establishing the connection between Moulthrop and Chandler is Chandler's portraits of the Reverend Dr. Devotion and his wife. That churchman had been associated with the Reverend Nicholas Street, who became Moulthrop's father-in-law, and it is probable that the future artist visited the Devotions and saw Chandler's portraits of them. Other members of the Devotion family who lived nearby had also been painted by Chandler, and Moulthrop probably saw these portraits as well. What does this all add up to? Simply that even relatively unsophisticated painters learned from one another. And if the speculation about Chandler's Boston apprenticeship is correct, the example of Copley and others filtered down through this visual grapevine. Moulthrop's work has a raw, primitive quality about it, but shows traces of style and sophistication as well. Perhaps the finest example of this is his portrait of the Reverend Ammi Ruhamah Robbins *(page 102)*. Seated comfortably at his library table, the Reverend Dr. Robbins—a distinguished educator and an early trustee of Williams College—is portrayed with fully convincing realism in a solid, three-dimensional setting. Comparisons with Chandler's work are obvious and the inspiration can even be traced to the early Copley manner.

William Sawitzky's ''discovery'' of the Moulthrop portraits, the artist's fragile connection with Chandler, and the fragments of his life story, have dozens of parallels in the archives of 18th and early 19th Century American art. Countless names have come to light in scattered portraits that show surprising skill. Until this century many of these names were written off as "primitives" whose lack of European training or of cosmopolitan reputation marked them as unworthy of serious study. While scores of art historians have devoted themselves to retracing the steps of the 16th Century Italian painter-author, Giorgio Vasari, who first described the lives of the artists of the Florentine Renaissance, the annals of early American art have remained largely blank.

For much of the work that has been done, we have to thank not institutions primarily devoted to the study of art, but state and county historical societies. Earl came to light largely as a result of the Connecticut Tercentenary of 1933. The state then became particularly aware of its history, and portraits of Connecticut notables by Earl began to tumble out of old houses and forgotten repositories. Much of the Sawitzkys' pioneering research on Moulthrop has been published by The New York Historical Society.

Provincialism and a bias for European art are not the only reasons why so many American painters of the late 18th Century are neglected, however. Perhaps the most serious handicap for even the most avid researcher is the sheer lack of information. For example, 40 years ago it was believed that three different artists bearing the name of Jennys—Richard, William and J. William—were all painting portraits in New England, especially around New Milford, Connecticut, in the late 1790s. J. William has, mercifully, been eliminated as a misreading of William's signature, but confusion persists regarding the other two despite a considerable body of work that bears the name Jennys. One of the several oddities in the story is that although Richard advertised the availability of his talent in the newspapers of Charleston, South Carolina, Savannah and New Haven, no painting by him has ever been found in those places. No documents of any kind mention William's name, but paintings signed and dated by him between 1795 and 1807 have shown up in Vermont, New Hampshire, Massachusetts and Connecticut. How Richard and William were related—if at all—no one knows.

A nd so it is with other painters of the period—Joseph Steward, John Durand, Rufus Hathaway—men whose work is known from too few examples and too few historical or biographical references. Different and distinctive enough so that even the untrained eye can identify their efforts after a brief exposure, they nevertheless share many characteristics. Primarily, of course, they are all portraitists—that is where trade took them. In painting faces, they almost all follow the rule of the itinerant, which is to get the job done as quickly and economically as possible, for speed is money. Thus, the style is spare, reduced to its essentials. Almost invariably, however, the likeness is good, perhaps slightly caricatured for emphasis, but recognizable: a frugal country patron would insist at least on that. And being rural faces, these are the stern, sharp, often guarded and accusatory visages of small-town folk; they are the New England conscience, drenched in the suspicion of sin, brought to life on canvas. The better painters, like the Jennyses, reveal their subjects with a solidity and strength, a sculptural quality that demonstrates not only a mastery of the medium —often as accomplished as Copley's—but a cool, unsentimental objectivity that has echoes in the very best American painting.

A young Connecticut matron, Hannah French Bacon, sat for her portrait by William Jennys in 1795. For the occasion she put on a splendid beribboned hat, an elaborate pleated collar and a taffeta dress belted with a buckled sash. From this and other signed Jennys pictures, it would seem that the artist preferred not to paint hands and that he tended to give sitters the same nose—marks of his limitations.

A People's Art

Among his contemporaries Copley shone like a meteor in a night sky. But when he sailed for Europe in 1774 he did not leave the American art scene entirely dark. Behind him a thriving tradition manifested itself in two ways. One group of painters, among them Reuben Moulthrop, Winthrop Chandler, Ralph Earl and John Durand, had access to metropolitan centers. Some may have seen Copley's portraits in Boston or New York and thus were able to base their work at least in part on skilled examples. Other painters, mostly anonymous rural craftsmen, continued to turn out a type of art as old as the original settlements—an unself-conscious art now labeled naïve, or folk, painting.

The products of these two mainstreams of American art have certain qualities in common. Their lack of pretension and their remarkable candor and directness may reflect the democratic spirit that pervaded the colonies even before the English yoke was thrown off. Their basic realism is perhaps an artistic expression of the down-to-earth pragmatism required by the rude necessities of everyday life at the time. Humor, too, punctuates these pictures, just as it leavened the early settlers' efforts simply to survive. All these characteristics are typical of American naïve painting in particular, but they also appear in the more sophisticated works, including those by Copley himself. They constitute the basic heritage of American art.

Not a portrait in the usual sense of a credible likeness, this is nevertheless a persuasive portrayal of Moses Marcy, a wealthy mill owner of Massachusetts. His neighbors would surely have recognized him from the artist's meticulous cataloguing of the "facts" of the subject's life: his shoreside home, his dog, pipe, account book, and a punch glass and bowl that may attest to Marcy's renown either as a host or as a drinker. Unskilled at depicting human features realistically, the anonymous artist chose instead to surround his sitter with a variety of personal references that add up to an effective visual biography.

Unknown: *Moses Marcy in a Landscape*, 1760

Unknown: *Mrs. Freake and Baby Mary*, c. 1674

WORCESTER ART MUSEUM, WORCESTER, MASSACHUSETTS, GIFT OF MR. AND MRS. ALBERT W. RICE, 1963

Unknown: *Ann Pollard*, 1721

Generations before Copley put brush to canvas, portraiture was known and appreciated by colonial settlers. Works like those shown here were produced by itinerant craftsmen, their names long since forgotten, or by local amateurs, men and women whose primitive way of life required the development of many different manual skills. Any housewife who could weave and dye her own cloth, design and cut a pattern, sew a dress and then embroider it, could certainly paint a picture.

Despite its faults of anatomy and perspective, the portrait of Mrs. Freake and her baby at left is not only an evocation of motherhood but a triumph of detail, notably in Mrs. Freake's fine lace collar and elegant skirt. The portrait of Ann Pollard above skillfully captures her piety and gives credence to the painter's claim that he made the picture in celebration of her 100th birthday.

Reuben Moulthrop: *Reverend Ammi Ruhamah Robbins,* date unknown

Winthrop Chandler: *Dr. William Glysson,* c. 1785

In the main, colonial portrait painters derived their patronage from that sturdy breed of Americans described as pillars of the community. Included in this category were not only the rich and the economically enterprising but—as shown here—doctors and ministers. The men charged with the physical and spiritual care of their fellows were proud of their professional status and happy to have it memorialized in paint.

The artists who produced the two portraits on this page, Reuben Moulthrop and Winthrop Chandler, were, unlike the Boston-bred Copley, essentially provincial in outlook. Moulthrop made a living by modeling wax effigies of well-known people and taking them on tour, as a sort of sideshow, through Pennsylvania, New York and Massachusetts. His skill at sculpting may explain the success of the three-dimensional effect in his study of a rural preacher, the Reverend Ammi Ruhamah Robbins *(top, left).* More convincing than most provincial portraits, it is also well composed, artfully designed —as in the patterning of the rug—and interestingly detailed. The attention Moulthrop lavished on the books perhaps stemmed from Robbins' desire to emphasize his erudition.

Chandler, who is believed to have started as a sign painter, apparently never traveled far from his Connecticut home. The portraits he produced are mostly of family and friends; Dr. William Glysson *(left),* shown still wearing his spurs while on a medical mission, was Chandler's brother-in-law. Both in this portrait and in an anonymous artist's rendition of Dr. Philomen Tracy *(opposite),* the subject's calling is proclaimed by posing him in the act of taking the pulse of an unseen patient. Although today's viewers may be baffled by this touch of mystery, colonial viewers were not. They knew that the patient in each case had to be a female, since the custom of the era decreed that women submitted to examination only while demurely concealed behind a curtain.

Unknown: *Dr. Philomen Tracy*, c. 1780

Attributed to John Durand: *Two Little Boys in a Garden*, c. 17

J ohn Durand is another of the several fairly well-known painters active during Copley's time. Reportedly French-born, Durand taught art in New York City and then traveled widely as a portraitist. The double portrait above is thought to be Durand's work. As their elders did when posing, these unidentified young boys wear their finest clothes, and fashionable periwigs as well.
In the portrait at right, the subject's identity is known but the artist's is not. Obviously, however, he had a strong sense of fantasy, for the gargantuan crystal goblet filled with luscious strawberries beside the child is a dream of delights. Perhaps the painter was simply showing off his skill at rendering translucent objects. While a trained painter would never have taken such license with reality, the exercise of the imagination is one of the hallmarks —and great charms—of the self-taught folk artist.

Unknown: *Emma van Name*, c. 1795

Although portraiture was the most profitable, it was not the only form of painting favored by America's early artists. Especially in the hinterlands, artisan-painters as well as amateurs busily produced landscapes, still lifes and sometimes scenes from the Bible or ancient history. In executing them the unfettered provincial felt bound by none of the conventions that restricted painters influenced by "high" European art.

The fascinating scene at the right is about as free and fanciful as one could ask. Among other things, it includes a vignette from American history, a Noah's arkful of animals, a tree-filled landscape and assorted cherubs. Its creator, Edward Hicks, was a coach and sign painter by trade, a Quaker minister by choice and, from the looks of his *The Peaceable Kingdom*, a confirmed eccentric. He produced some 100 versions of this picture, all loosely derived from an English engraving whose Biblical theme, based on the 11th chapter of Isaiah, preached universal brotherhood. Hicks's own embellishments on the theme sometimes included a scene *(lower left background)* showing William Penn, his illustrious Quaker ancestor, making his famous treaty with the Indians.

106

Edward Hicks: *The Peaceable Kingdom*, c. 1840

Unknown: *The Cat*, c. 1840

The inventiveness and imagination that Hicks displayed in his *Peaceable Kingdom* were typical of the unabashed vitality of naïve American art. Painters who, like Copley, fixed their gaze on European traditions would never have ventured such uninhibited blendings of real life, fantasy, history and allegory. But the folk painter brooked no restraints. The pictures on these pages wonderfully exemplify this freedom of attitude. They are not only portraits of animals—no proper Boston patron or painter would have sanctioned such works—but they are portraits with a difference. The picture of the cat above, painted by an unknown New York artist, is less a likeness of a particular animal than a study of *catness*—the essence of the feline character. It is, moreover, a bird's-eye view of a cat—a startlingly graphic avian nightmare.

The painting at the right is a more conventional

108

D. G. Stouter: *On Point*, c. 1840

representation. Here is a specific dog, perhaps the artist's own favorite hunting companion. Unfortunately, all that is known about the painter is that his (or her) name was D. G. Stouter; the picture is signed thus in the lower left corner. But there is no doubting Stouter's artistic talents: the pointer is handsome and clear-eyed and the quail are the kind of lively, full-bodied birds any hunter would love to bag. Adding to the picture's

interest is the fact that the focus is from the ground, making the dog seem a bit more short-legged than he should be, but suggesting the point of view of the prey.

Although these pictures are not categorized as so-called "fine" art, they possess two qualities that would do any painter proud: they obviously exploit all the resources at the artist's command, and their intentions are both perfectly clear and perfectly fulfilled.

The landscapes and still lifes produced by the naïve painters were not generally considered "acceptable" subjects for the academy-minded artist, and they were not widely taken up by professional American painters until the middle of the 19th Century.

This staggering feast of fruits seems to have been painted in New Jersey by an artist known only as Wagguno. In all likelihood, he had seen examples of sophisticated American or European art, for the device of framing a landscape in a window at the background of a scene was commonly emphasized in Continental paintings, and indeed even in Copley's work. In most respects, though, the painting is as inept as it is charming. The grapes at the left, for example, are surely doomed to slip off the table. The wire basket behind the watermelon floats freely in space. The chirping goldfinch is bound to fall from its perch if it has to hold its balance for more than a second. But it is too easy to find fault with this painting, as it is with the others on previous pages. What is more challenging—and more to the point—is to find the qualities that make these paintings succeed, and simply to enjoy their success.

Wagguno: *Fruit and Goldfinch*, 1858

V

The Pennsylvania Prodigy

Many paradoxes mark the life of the painter who first encouraged Copley to leave America, but the most interesting is that he became a painter at all. For Benjamin West was reared as a Quaker, one of the gentle people, whose tenets forbade art in church and frowned on it elsewhere as a useless, if not immoral, activity. But the Quakers had—and still have—another belief that helps resolve the paradox: a man, they say, must follow his Inner Light, and if the Inner Light leads him to draw and paint, then he must do so. And West, it is claimed, was moved to draw and paint from the age of six on.

He was born near Philadelphia on September 10, 1738, some two months after Copley was born in Boston. His birthplace was an inn owned by his father in Springfield Township, on what is now the campus of Swarthmore College. The inn was one of a succession that John West owned, none apparently very profitable.

Most of what is known of West's early life comes from information the artist himself gave to a contemporary and not entirely reliable biographer, John Galt. Among the stories Galt relayed are that West had his first lesson in mixing paints from friendly Indians, that he made so many paintbrushes from the fur of the family cat that his father thought the poor beast had caught the mange, and that at six Benjamin spontaneously drew a perfect likeness of his baby niece—a feat deemed so marvelous that, Quaker injunctions or not, he was encouraged to paint flowers, birds or anything his precocious eye fancied.

When West was about eight, a prosperous Philadelphia relative, Edward Penington, stopped at the family inn, saw the boy's pictures and was so impressed that he sent him some paints and engravings. Shortly afterward, he took Benjamin to Philadelphia to meet one of the city's few resident artists, an extraordinary man named William Williams. Among his varied gifts, Williams was a novelist, an adventurer, and owner of a night school where he taught drawing and music, coincidentally somewhat like the school run in Boston by Copley's stepfather. Williams advertised that he did painting to order, including "history, portrait, landskip, sign painting, lettering and gilding." The portraits by him that survive have a clutter of detail and rather awkward anatomy, but little Benjamin West must have found them wonderful.

The impressionable youngster probably got a great deal more from Williams' library. He was able to peruse the same books that Copley inherited from his stepfather, Fresnoy's *The Art of Painting* and Richardson's *The Theory of Painting*. Among other principles that West took to heart and never forgot was Richardson's thesis that painting was a universal language that transcended the barriers of speech, and that art "pours ideas into our minds, [while] words only drop them." West's later tendency to rationalize and moralize in his paintings surely had its origin in these early readings.

In the years after his meeting with Williams and his first sight of Philadelphia's oil paintings, West began to earn small sums by producing portraits of local gentlemen on commission. Evidently he was quick to show his gifts, for at 16 he was well enough regarded to be invited to journey to Lancaster to paint a portrait of William Henry, a wealthy gunsmith.

Literate and discerning, Henry watched the progress of his portrait and was so taken with both the artist and his skill that he offered a suggestion: West ought to paint historical pictures rather than merely portraits. As Galt tells the story, the young painter was extremely flattered but confessed that he did not understand what was meant by history painting. Thereupon Henry pulled a book from his library shelf and read aloud an account of the death of Socrates. West, enchanted, hurried off to translate the scene into a sketch, perhaps guided by an engraving in the book. The drawing that resulted was rough, but so pleased Henry that he promptly asked West to base a painting on it. *The Death of Socrates* became West's first effort at the kind of painting that was to secure his fame: a work crowded with figures, based on a theme from the past.

West's stay at Lancaster produced an unexpected benefit, a meeting with still another of the many intelligent, well-placed, generous men who were to be crucial to him at every stage of his career. William Smith, Provost of the College of Philadelphia, happened to be lecturing in Lancaster while West was working for Henry. Evidently he found the young painter unusually likable and sincere; in any event, like West's other benefactors he was moved to help him out of purely selfless motives. He invited West to study at the college he headed in Philadelphia. Established by Benjamin Franklin, the first in America not founded as a theological school, it eventually became the University of Pennsylvania. Of most import for West, Smith seemed to know exactly the kind of schooling a budding painter needed. He shunted his new charge away from the traditional emphasis on Latin and Greek grammar but grounded him in classical mythology and history. He seems also to have urged West to take as his major guide the admonition he had already read in Richardson's book on painting—"that which is most beautiful is the most noble subject." The stress Smith's instruction placed on antiquity and high-mindedness was to serve West well in later years, not only in themes for his paintings, but in the generally rational approach that distinguished his art.

For several years West earned a living as a portraitist in Philadelphia, then spent a year in New York; like Copley, he found a lively and higher-priced market for his talents there. But with growing success came boredom. Having seen everything that Philadelphia and New York could offer in the way of art, he longed, again like Copley, to branch out. With his brief but happy taste of history painting, a pilgrimage to the Old World, to Italy in particular, seemed to him a must if he were to feel truly secure as an artist. Again help came from an older man. Provost Smith had introduced him to a wealthy Philadelphia merchant and judge, William Allen (later founder of the city of Allentown). In 1759, when West was 21, Allen arranged passage for him aboard a ship bound for Italy with wheat and flour exported by Allen's firm.

On July 10, 1760, West saw Rome for the first time—and was horrified. As his biographer Galt puts it: "In America all was young, vigorous and growing. In Rome, all was old, infirm and decaying, the autumn of a people who had gathered their glory and were sinking in sleep under the dreadful excesses of the vintage." Moreover, West was dismayed by the paintings he saw, by what seemed an excess not only of Catholic but pagan themes. Reared in Quaker austerity, he felt assaulted by Rome's papal splendor, the ostentation of its baroque architecture, the awesome grandeur of its classical past. He was offended, as well, by the hordes of beggars on Rome's streets, and by the overfed elegance of its aristocrats.

The engraving above, showing a fragment of a Greek urn that depicts the blind Oedipus being led out of his kingdom of Thebes, is from *Monumenti Antichi Inediti*, one of the major works of the great 18th Century German scholar Johann Winckelmann. The virtual founder of classical archeology, Winckelmann also made significant contributions to the methodical study of art history and styles. The portrait of him below is by his chief disciple and exponent, the painter Anton Raphael Mengs.

As always, however, he was lucky in the friendships he made. Soon after his arrival he met Thomas Robinson, an English esthete living in Rome, who was so charmed by the Quaker innocent that he undertook to introduce him to the city's art colony. One of its leading tastemakers, an eminent patron of the arts, was Alessandro Cardinal Albani. Though blind, Albani was a perceptive connoisseur. On appraising West with his sensitive hands—as he also evaluated sculpture, medals and reliefs—the cardinal declared that he had a fine head and should make a distinguished artist. This was all the sycophantic Roman patrons needed to hear. West was wined and dined and escorted around town as if he were the new Raphael—and he had not yet set brush to canvas.

Probably the most influential person West met during his three-year stay in Rome was Anton Raphael Mengs, shortly to become chief court painter to the King of Spain and now leading practitioner of the style that was soon to sweep Europe—Neoclassicism. Mengs took West under his wing, but when he saw a portrait West had painted of Thomas Robinson as a demonstration of his abilities, he conceded that he could teach the young American little in the way of technique. He did, however, set West to copying both the works in his studio and numbers of old masters in collections in Rome, Florence, Bologna and Venice.

Most important of all, West was indoctrinated in the theories of Mengs's celebrated fellow German Johann Joachim Winckelmann. Archeologist, esthetician, lawgiver to a whole generation of artists, Winckelmann was then in charge of the excavations at Pompeii and Herculaneum, two port towns of the old Roman Empire, whose rediscovery, respectively in 1709 and 1748, had stimulated a passionate European revival of interest in the classical era. Winckelmann was occupied at the digs during West's Roman sojourn, but West was able to learn of his theories both through Mengs and through another friend he acquired in Rome, the Scottish painter Gavin Hamilton. In essence, Winckelmann's thinking reflected the poet Alexander Pope's dictum that "the proper study of mankind is man." Winckelmann believed that man could be most properly studied only in his most heroic and illuminating aspects, and that nowhere were these qualities more manifest than in the civilizations of ancient Greece and Rome. As to art, Winckelmann felt that it must imitate nature. But, he insisted, the most nearly perfect imitations of nature ever produced were those of ancient sculpture; therefore, the artist must learn to imitate nature not by looking at nature but by imitating ancient statues.

His disciples, Mengs most prominent among them, summed up Winckelmann's artistic credo in a slogan that echoed everywhere in their work: noble simplicity and calm grandeur. It is an eminently rational slogan, and the works of art produced in response to it are eminently rational in mood and structure. By the time West left Italy for England in August of 1763 he had fully absorbed the new philosophy and the new style.

He intended to stay only a short while in London en route back to Pennsylvania, but the English capital, as it had for many colonials, proved irresistible. It was to be West's home henceforth; he never again saw America. After his arrival he met Joshua Reynolds, Thomas Gainsborough, Richard Wilson and other prominent painters and set up his own studio. That winter he also made a profound, if unintended, impression on London society by demonstrating his skill as a fancy skater on the frozen lagoon of Kensington Gardens. West's expertise, acquired on the Schuylkill River in Philadelphia, caught the attention of London's sporting elements, who perhaps reasoned that anyone who could cut so fine a figure on the ice could probably do as well on canvas. The painter's studio rapidly filled with curious visitors, although not yet with buyers. Like the native British painters, West suffered for a while from the preference of most English patrons for works by Continental hands.

Within a year after settling in London, West had not only exhibited with the Society of Artists but had taken a bride. She was a young lady he had known in Philadelphia, Elizabeth Shewell, and there are two very different accounts of how they came to be married. By far the better story is that Elizabeth's brother, who was also her guardian, had actually locked her in her room when he learned that West had urged her to come to London to marry him, and that some of West's friends, Benjamin Franklin included, had arranged for her escape via a rope ladder, a midnight coach, and a secret sailing—in the best tradition of the operatic comedies of the time. The second story, as told by Matthew Pratt, a pupil of West's, is that far from opposing the marriage, Elizabeth's brother had had her escorted to Europe by Pratt and West's father. As if to lend the story still more decorum, Pratt declared that both he and old Mr. West had gone along on the honeymoon.

West supported his new wife and London household by painting portraits. The opportunity he wanted to paint grand themes from history finally came from a formidable patron indeed: Robert Hay Drummond, Archbishop of York. The painting he commissioned—*Agrippina with the Ashes of Germanicus (pages 121-122)*—is based on a story in the *An-*

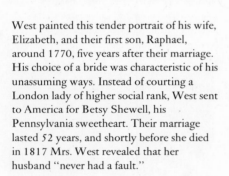

West painted this tender portrait of his wife, Elizabeth, and their first son, Raphael, around 1770, five years after their marriage. His choice of a bride was characteristic of his unassuming ways. Instead of courting a London lady of higher social rank, West sent to America for Betsy Shewell, his Pennsylvania sweetheart. Their marriage lasted 52 years, and shortly before she died in 1817 Mrs. West revealed that her husband "never had a fault."

nals of Tacitus that the archbishop felt epitomized the theme of moral uprightness. Germanicus, a First Century Roman general and member of the imperial family, who had defeated the German barbarians on the Rhine and so earned his nickname, had become so popular that the jealous Emperor Tiberius had him transferred to Syria and poisoned there. Germanicus' wife, Agrippina, had his body cremated and set sail back to Italy to bury the ashes in sacred soil. When her landing place became known, many officers who had served under her husband gathered with their families and friends to pay their final respects. As Agrippina and her two children stepped off the ship carrying the funerary urn, a great cry of grief burst from the multitude. West's painting of this scene perfectly fulfills the ideal of art set forth by Winckelmann: its theme and treatment are heroic, the stately widow who defies an emperor to honor her husband's memory is a model of moral courage, and the viewer is presumably uplifted by her noble act.

The archbishop, who had carefully discussed with West how the scene should be depicted, was delighted with the result. So convinced was he that West's métier lay in such historical works that he tried to raise a fund that would permit the artist to devote full time to them. Failing this, he prevailed upon King George III to examine the painting, knowing that if His Majesty liked it, royal patronage would soon flow West's way. He gauged his monarch well, for immediately upon seeing the painting the King asked West to paint one for him. In fact, according to Galt's biography of West, the King could scarcely contain his enthusiasm; he promptly sent for a copy of Livy's *History of Rome* and, in his own royal voice, deigned to read the story of the noble Roman general Regulus, proposing this as the theme for West to paint.

Galt's tale of the royal reading is inaccurate, but the meeting between George III and West did take place, and King and commoner became unusually close friends. George III was rightly called the "Farmer King"; his tastes in art, as in other matters, were simple and unsophisticated. West's country upbringing and modest Quaker mien strongly appealed to him, and the relationship they formed was probably more intimate than any that has ever existed between a royal patron and an artist. West was given studios in royal residences both in London and at Windsor where the King could spend hours with him discussing artistic projects.

It is safe to assume that some of their early conversations centered on the establishment of an official academy of the arts. By now West knew most of England's leading painters, and undoubtedly shared their feeling that the nation's art needed august backing. The existing artists' societies in London were still shakily organized and financed, and lacked adequate exhibition rooms. On December 10, 1768, George III changed all this by establishing the Royal Academy of Arts and giving it headquarters at an old royal residence, Somerset House. Subsidized by the Crown, the Academy was to have a top rank of 40 artists, no more, no less, in perpetuity, representing the best of British painters, sculptors and architects. Moreover, the Academy was empowered to open a school for the instruction of worthy young talents. On the list of the Academy's founders West's name is second, preceded only by that of Joshua Reynolds. When

Reynolds' death ended his long reign as the Academy's first president, West succeeded him.

Over the years West executed some 75 paintings and designs for paintings for George III: history paintings, religious paintings, portraits of the Royal Family, scenes from the lives of English monarchs. The most grandiose scheme that King and painter conjured up was a plan for 36 huge paintings on the theme of "Revealed Religion, from its commencement to its completion" to be hung in a projected new chapel in Windsor Castle; as it turned out only seven of the paintings were completed. Of greater moment to art history, West's 32 years of royal commissions saw a series of transformations both in the style of his art and in the subjects he emphasized. The first of these changes—one that generated intense controversy—appeared in 1771, with his painting of *The Death of Wolfe (pages 126-127)*.

Wolfe, one of the most popular British commanders of his time, had been killed two years earlier at the moment of his victory in the Battle of Quebec, which effectively smashed the power of France in Canada. West's painting of the event is quite within the convention of the day except in one startling respect: rather than showing Wolfe and his soldiers in classical garb, as custom dictated, he clothed them in contemporary uniform.

Galt's biography has it that the Archbishop of York was so agitated at this uncharacteristic defiance of convention that he brought Reynolds to see West's picture while it still was in progress. Reynolds urged his colleague "earnestly to adopt the classic costume of antiquity as much more becoming the inherent greatness of the subject than the modern garb of war." West argued that the event had taken place very recently, "in a region of the world unknown to the Greeks and Romans, and at a period of time when no such nations, nor heroes in their costumes, any longer existed. . . . It is a topic that history will proudly record, and the same truth that guides the pen of the historian should govern the pencil of the artist."

West, however, agreed to be guided by Reynolds' opinion after he had seen the finished work. In due course, Reynolds and the archbishop returned to see the completed canvas. Reynolds seated himself before the picture and examined it closely for about half an hour. He then rose and declared, "Mr. West has conquered."

Actually, Reynolds did not give in that easily. The following year, when *The Death of Wolfe* was on display at the Royal Academy's annual exhibition, Reynolds returned to the attack in one of his now-celebrated discourses, propounding an idea that falls quaintly indeed upon modern ears. "Works . . . which are built upon general nature live forever," he declared, "while those which depend for their existence on particular customs and habits, a partial view of nature, or the fluctuation of fashion, can only be coeval with that which first raised them from obscurity. Present time and future may be considered as rivals, and he who solicits the one must expect to be discountenanced by the other."

Despite Reynolds' prediction, *The Death of Wolfe* proved a sensation at the Academy. In later years West returned repeatedly to the theme of the heroic military death told in contemporary terms. One of his most rousing combat scenes is *The Battle of La Hogue (pages 128-131)*; the

King kindly provided research help by sending West out on a ship of the line in the company of an admiral, while part of the royal fleet maneuvered in the wind and fired blank charges. West also produced two versions of *The Death of Lord Nelson,* and a distinctly overstuffed *Apotheosis of Nelson,* intended as a monument in Westminster Abbey. Undoubtedly nearer to the heart of the Quaker from Pennsylvania was his recording of a nonmilitary event of recent history, the convincingly realistic *Penn's Treaty with the Indians (page 123).*

THE PHILADELPHIA MUSEUM OF ART

If West startled viewers with his insistence on using contemporary costume, he also worried his admirers by gradually abandoning the Neoclassical style on which his early fame rested. The new style he evolved —the critic Grose Evans has described it as West's "Dread Manner" —delved into the darker world of man's imagination and irrationality. In a sense it dealt with the underside, the complementary mirror image, of Neoclassical rationalism—an approach that made West a direct precursor of the English and French Romantic artists of the 19th Century. West developed this style while pursuing the ambitious series of paintings on "Revealed Religion" that he and George III had envisioned for the royal chapel at Windsor Castle. The paintings were not only to be imposingly large, but heavily oriented toward miraculous happenings, as indicated in the titles of some of the works: *Moses and His Brother Aaron Before Pharaoh, Their Rods Turned into Serpents; Moses Showing the Brazen Serpent to the Infirm to be Healed (page 124); Saul and the Witch of Endor.* Perhaps the most important of the lot is *Death on a Pale Horse,* based on a Biblical theme, a painting in which West attempted to generate awe and terror by the use of heavy colors, veiled figures, violent action and bolts of lightning. He went on to apply this "Dread Manner" in works based on literary themes, including Spenser's *Faerie Queen* and a number of Shakespeare's plays.

In turning to the irrational, West found a powerful ally in Edmund Burke, author of the enormously influential treatise *A Philosophical Inquiry into the Origins of our Ideas on the Sublime and the Beautiful.* This work, published by Burke in 1756, had created a furor among thinking men and was to prove a bible of its own to later Romantic artists. Burke, in essence, called for a reaction against the cool rationalism of thought that had dominated 18th Century life up to that time and that had produced the Neoclassical style in art. Instead, he argued for a reign of emotion, of individual feeling. In art, Burke said, this would manifest itself in quiet pleasure over the Beautiful—which he defined as the smooth, the soft in color, the small in size—and in exaltation over the Sublime—which he defined as the large, the dark, the rough and the mysterious.

West's interpretation of this manifesto in various paintings won gradual acceptance from his admirers, but the innovation they came to prefer —the one that modern viewers also most favor in West's work—was his contemporary treatment of contemporary history. It was in this arena that he met his major challenge from the compatriot he had generously befriended. From 1775 on, when Copley arrived in London to settle, the battle between the two Americans was to resound throughout the British art world for nearly three decades.

Foreshadowing the Romantic era in art, Benjamin West's *Death on a Pale Horse* is the most dramatic exposition of his late style, in which the dark, irrational side of man's nature is vividly pictured. The painting is based on the Revelation of St. John the Divine. In the detail above from an oil sketch for the work, Death, his wild eyes gleaming, gallops roughshod out of the shadows as humanity falls helplessly before him.

The King's Painter

When Benjamin West arrived in London in 1763 after three years of study in Italy, he won almost instant success, establishing a fame that continued for most of the rest of his long life. Permanently settled in England, the American-born painter enjoyed unusual prestige and reward. For nearly three decades he served as president of the Royal Academy. He became a warm personal friend of King George III, received some 75 royal commissions, many of them huge, wall-covering canvases, and earned more than £34,000 in fees from the Crown alone.

Everything his fellow expatriate Copley strove so hard for—court patronage, financial security, public recognition—seemed to come easily to West. Part of the reason for this may be that the Pennsylvania Quaker was immensely likable. A pleasant-looking, fair-haired man, he dressed and acted modestly, spoke with sincerity and radiated a friendly enthusiasm that must have been appealing. West's popularity was also due to his skill at painting large, busy scenes from history—Biblical, classical and contemporary—that had satisfying overtones of moral uplift and patriotic zeal. Starting with the Neoclassical style he had learned in Italy, he also employed a realism so straightforward it shocked some of his colleagues, and in some vividly dramatic religious works he anticipated the Romanticism that swept European art after his death.

In this detail from West's first major English painting *(following page)*, the Roman noblewoman Agrippina, accompanied by her children and attendants, carries an urn containing the ashes of her popular warrior husband, Germanicus. Her gesture is an act of defiance, for Germanicus had been assassinated by order of his jealous emperor and had been denied a hero's funeral. In its noble simplicity and calm grandeur, West's painting fulfills the two basic requirements of the Neoclassical style.

Agrippina Landing at Brundisium with the Ashes of Germanicus, detail, 1768

Agrippina Landing at Brundisium with the Ashes of Germanicus, 176?

Initially West busied himself in London painting portraits. But he considered this mere potboiling and yearned for the opportunity to devote his skills to more important subjects, especially historical scenes that embodied the theme of courage. His first big chance came in 1766, when the Archbishop of York asked him to base a painting on the writings of the ancient Roman historian Tacitus. The prelate himself selected a suitable passage, and the resulting work, *Agrippina Landing at Brundisium with the Ashes of Germanicus (above)*, is a perfect example

of the Neoclassical principles West admired. To help achieve the symmetry and harmony of his composition, he used a device called the "bridge formula," placing the main figures—Agrippina, her attendants and children—in a kind of frieze, with empty space between them and the viewer. In the lower corners of the painting are subordinate figures whose attitudes and actions direct the eye to the central group.

Several years later, when West turned to subjects from more recent history, he was still using the "bridge

Penn's Treaty with the Indians, 1771

formula" and well-balanced Neoclassical style. In the picture above, he depicted an event that must have been especially dear to his Quaker heart. According to legend, William Penn, who founded Pennsylvania as an American haven for the Quakers, negotiated a treaty with the Indians in 1682 which assured them equal rights and freedoms in the territory. There is no real evidence that such a treaty was ever made, but belief in the story persisted and West preserved it in paint. Since he lacked documentation for the scene—except for the costume and look of the Indians and the appearance of Penn, which was known—West included portraits of his father and his stepbrother, Thomas, who stands behind Penn.

West viewed the painting as a pictorial statement of the virtues of human rectitude. In a letter written in 1805, he explained that "the great object I had in forming that composition, was to express savages brought into harmony and piece by justice and benevolance, by not withholding from them what was their right, and giving to them what they were in want of."

Angel of the Lord Announcing the Resurrection to the Marys at the Sepulchre, 1805

The Brazen Serpent, 1790

West departed from the Neoclassical style to some extent when he painted subjects from contemporary history, but he broke with it completely when he worked with Biblical themes later in his career. His new style—described by one scholar as his "Dread Manner"—differs from the Neoclassical in mood, composition and the treatment of figures. Moreover, these pictures appeal not to the viewer's reason but primarily to his emotions; their aim is to evoke awe and fear.

In the paintings shown here, West has abandoned the "bridge formula," with its row of figures neatly arranged across the middle ground. A sense of order has given way to a sense of movement, generated by sharp contrasts of light and shadow and a billowing disarray of draperies, hair and clouds. The mood is no longer serene, but turbulent. In the painting at top left, the central figure is a wild-eyed angel *(detail, right)* who announces Christ's Resurrection to the three Marys. In the painting at left, an angry Moses confronts his people as they writhe amid serpents sent to punish them for their impiety. He points to a bronze serpent—a symbol of healing—and exhorts them to do the Lord's will.

This huge painting—more than 12 feet high—is one of a series on "Revealed Religion" that George III commissioned West to paint for a projected chapel at Windsor Castle. To avoid charges of "popery" from the conservative Church of England hierarchy, West took pains to consult with ecclesiastical authorities before setting brush to canvas. With the King's help he got their approval, but before the long project could be completed His Majesty had begun to go insane, and his grandiose scheme for the chapel was abandoned. The paintings were returned to West, although he had already been paid some £20,000 for his years of work.

The Death of Wolfe, painted about a decade after the event it commemorated, was West's most popular work. General James Wolfe's victory over the French at Quebec, securing Britain's hold on Canada, had stirred great national pride. Wolfe and his men had scaled a precipitous height to gain the Plains of Abraham behind the city, and there shot it out toe to toe with a superior French force led by General Louis Joseph de Montcalm. Standing in the midst of his troops, Wolfe was twice wounded, then fatally hit by a third musket ball. As he lay bleeding, he heard one of his officer's exclaim that the enemy was giving way in all directions. "Now I die contented," said Wolfe, and calmly expired.

West was at first heavily criticized for depicting his figures in contemporary dress. When the King heard of the painter's plan he is reported to have observed that it was "very ridiculous to exhibit heroes in coats, breeches and cock'd hats." But West argued that it was equally ridiculous to show modern men in togas and armor, and he won the day.

In spite of its realistic details —down to the body paint on the Indian—the picture is not entirely factual. It is believed that Wolfe died with only three men near him. But a number of other officers may have convinced the artist that they had seen their commander die; the story goes that they wanted to be included in West's painting and gave him £100 apiece for the privilege. In any case, the picture won such applause that West painted five versions of it. One of them was claimed by the King, despite his previous critique.

The Death of Wolfe, 1770

127

Eight years after celebrating British military prowess on land in *The Death of Wolfe,* West painted a historic victory at sea in *The Battle of La Hogue (details, following pages).*

In 1692 the English were threatened with invasion by an army mounted by their deposed Catholic monarch, James II, in France. British ships destroyed some of the French fleet and drove the remainder into the bay of La Hogue, which was protected by massive land-based artillery. Unable to sail into the anchorage, the English pursued their attack in small boats. Led by Vice-Admiral George Rooke *(standing in the boat at the left),* they rowed in at night, fought their way onto the enemy ships, turned the guns around and destroyed the shore artillery. At one point during the battle, James II forgot his enmity and cried out: "See my brave English sailors!"

West's painting was widely cheered at its exhibition in 1780, but trouble loomed. Some viewers detected a note of sympathy for James in the work, cited West's avowed approval of the American and French Revolutions, and questioned his loyalty to the Crown. The criticism did not prevent West's election in 1792 as president of the Royal Academy, but eventually it started up again. As George III became increasingly unstable, West lost his prestige at court. His last years were spent in decline, with only the echoes of successes like *The Battle of La Hogue* to comfort him.

The Battle of La Hogue, 1778

VI

Rivalry
in London

Copley made his bid for entry into the most exclusive circle of British painters—those patronized by George III and the aristocracy —with this fanciful portrait of the King's three youngest daughters. Despite its vitality and freshness, and the delicate floral still life at the lower right that demonstrated Copley's talent beyond portraiture, the work was vilified by classically oriented critics, chiefly for its busy rococo air. Copley's failure took on tragic overtones later the same year when two of his own children died of minor diseases.

The Three Youngest Daughters of King George III, 1785

The ship that carried Copley from Boston to England on the eve of the American Revolution made port at Deal on July 9, 1774. His dream of seeing the Old World at last a reality, the 36-year-old artist at once began to record his reactions in a long series of letters home, most of them to Sukey, his wife, and to his half brother, Henry. The letters were compounded equally of enthusiasm and anxiety, shrewdness and naïveté, and they were full of sharp-eyed observations.

From Deal, Copley rode to London in a post chaise, a public conveyance "as genteel as any Chariot that roals through your Streets, with a Postillion well Dress'd as any you have seen in the service of the first gentlemen of fortune among you . . . and this Journey of 72 Miles cost me but three Guineas." Promptly on his arrival in the British capital he "procured some things to be Decent in" and then called on his compatriot and correspondent Benjamin West and on Sir Joshua Reynolds who, as first president of the Royal Academy, had been knighted in 1768. In West's company Copley visited the Royal Academy, where for the first time he saw students drawing from a nude model. He greatly admired the Academy's collection of sculpture and painting, and was especially taken with West's *Death of Wolfe*. On the basis of this survey, he confidently concluded that "the practice of Painting or rather the means by which composition is attained is easier than I thought it had been."

As for London itself, Copley found it "really an astonishing City: many parts of which, I mean the buildings, are so exactly what I had conceived that I am surprised at it." He also remarked on the "great deal of Manly politeness in the English." West invited him to dine whenever he had a free evening, and Reynolds personally showed him some of the sights of the city.

But enchanted as he was with the British and their capital, Copley was eager to move on to Italy. He had several offers to do portraits in London, but he turned them down, preferring to pursue his studies in Italy. West was highly encouraging, assuring him that on the Continent he "need coppy very little, that fifteen Months for me will be equel to as many years to young Students." After six weeks in London a lighthearted

Copley set out across the Channel with a British painter he had met, George Carter, who was not only an experienced traveler but had the advantage of speaking French and Italian.

From Paris, their first stop, Copley reported what subsequent generations of American tourists have often reaffirmed—that "there is something in the air of France that accelerates, or quickens, the circulation of the fluids of the human body." He had much to report about the French way of life—the wines, he wrote home chauvinistically, were "not so strong as our Cyder"—but he had even more to say about French art. At the cathedral of Notre Dame—"a very Beautiful Pile of Gothick Architecture"—he was profoundly moved by the dramatic marble *Pietà* group behind the main altar, the work of the 18th Century sculptor Nicolas Coustou. Copley particularly marveled at Coustou's flowing rendition in stone of a piece of linen draped behind the figures of the dead Christ and His grieving mother. The drapery, he wrote, "plays off from the group and as a flame loses itself . . . into a readish soft colour that tapers into many serpentine streaming points and gently steals unperceived into reaths of Smoke, so in this manner the mass is melted away." Relating this technique in stone to his own art, he observed that "all lights in Pictures aught to be so managed. the first great Light ought to be followed by some succeeding ones less powerful . . . that lets the eye off by gentle degrees. this is effected by Colours as well as lights and shades."

Copley's education continued at the Luxembourg Palace. There he scrutinized paintings by Peter Paul Rubens, noting the easy, vibrant lines of the figures and a distribution of colors so deft that the effect was "one agreeable whole, pertakeing of many tints so well proportioned to each other that none predominates." The provincial was learning fast. West had estimated that he would need more than a year to absorb the lessons of Europe, but he mastered some of them in two months. He would gradually reform the chief characteristics, the strongly contrasting colors and precise contours, of his American works.

His education in human relations was less successful. As he and Carter pushed on toward Italy, their friendship rapidly deteriorated. The story did not come out until some 50 years later, with the publication of passages from Carter's diary in Allan Cunningham's *Lives of Most Eminent British Painters and Sculptors*. According to Cunningham, Copley viewed Carter as "a sort of snail which crawled over a man in his sleep and left its slime and no more." Carter, in turn, described Copley as "very thin, pale, a little pock-marked, prominent eyebrows, small eyes, which, after fatigue, seemed a day's march in his head."

What irked the Englishman, however, was not Copley's unprepossessing appearance but his behavior. "My agreeable companion," he wrote irately, "suspects he has got a cold upon his lungs. He is now sitting by a fire, the heat of which makes me very faint, a silk handkerchief about his head, and a white pocket one about his neck, applying fresh fuel, and complaining that the wood of this country don't give half the heat that the wood of America does . . . He never asked me yet, and we have been up an hour, how I do, or how I passed the night: 'tis an engaging creature."

To Carter, obviously, Copley was no more than a boorish American know-it-all, lacking in the "Manly politeness" that Copley himself had admired in the English. The opinion is important primarily because in time it was to be shared by many of Carter's countrymen. Copley's self-absorption, as well as his habit of looking out for the main chance, were to count heavily against him in the ultimate failure of his London career.

For all their annoyance with each other, the ill-matched travelers continued on together and in October 1774 reached Genoa, which Copley said made Boston seem like a collection of wren boxes. From there a letter to his wife mentioned for the first time the possibility of her joining him upon his return to England: "If in three or four years I can make as much as will render the rest of our life easy, and leave something to our family if I should be called away, I believe that you would think it best to spend that time there; should this be done, be assured, I am ready to promise you that I will go back and enjoy that domestic happiness which our little 'farm' is capable of affording. I am sure you would like England very much; it is a very paradise; but so I think is Boston Common, if the town is what it once was."

Copley's foreboding about his native city was justified. Arriving in Rome several weeks later, he found a letter from his wife reporting that British troops had occupied Boston and Beacon Hill, where the Copley estate was located, and that the situation had become so tense that she was planning to join him abroad with their children.

Although anxious for his family and worried over the fate of his farm, Copley could not suppress his elation at being in Rome at last. He soon separated from Carter and, with the help of the Scottish painter Gavin Hamilton, found lodgings. He also took up with a number of English-speaking artists and intellectuals who frequented a Roman tavern called the English Coffee House, and he launched on an energetic program of sightseeing and study. Up at eight each morning, he would hurry out to visit the Vatican and St. Peter's, the Capitol and other landmarks. The architecture and the sculpture enraptured him, and so did the paintings of Italy's old masters, until now known to him only through copies or his reading. After long hours spent contemplating and analyzing them, Copley decided that "they exceed description." Still, they did not overawe him. Ebullient as ever, he wrote to his wife: "I know the extent of the arts, to what lengths they have been carried, and I feel more confidence in what I do myself than before I came."

The immediate result of that surge of confidence was a picture that Copley would never have attempted in Puritan Boston, with its old taboo on church art. Copley's theme was the Ascension of Christ; he labored for three months on this first production in Europe, his first original venture outside the field of portraiture. As it happens, we have step-by-step details of how he went about this work. Back in Boston, his half brother, Henry, had recently begun to paint on his own, and Copley apparently thought it would be instructive to explain the process to him at length.

In planning *The Ascension,* he wrote Pelham, he decided "to carry the figures (of the Disciples and angels) in a circle which would suppose a place that Christ stood. This I fixed before I determined the disposition of a single figure, as I knew it would make a fine breadth of light and shadow and give a Grand appearance to the whole: and I am certain Raphael pursued a Method something like this." Once the basic composition was set, Copley made a preliminary drawing of the picture. He sketched figures in action by using himself as a model, posing in front of a mirror; to visualize the fall of draperies, he arranged a damp tablecloth on a "layman," an artist's dummy about three feet tall. Satisfied at last with his preliminary drawing, he transferred it to canvas and hired a model to pose for the heads, hands and feet.

When *The Ascension* was finished Copley proudly relayed some high praise for it to Pelham. His fellow painter Gavin Hamilton, he wrote, had said that "he never saw a finer Composition in his life and that he knows of no one who can equil it." But since the canvas measured only 32 by 29 inches, Hamilton urged Copley to do a larger version of it, the better to establish his reputation in Europe. Copley, however, did not want to take time from his studies; besides, he hoped that someday a church might commission a life-sized *Ascension* for an altarpiece. "To paint it as large as life," the artist wrote Pelham, "would take a Canvis 24 feet by 18, so I cannot do that unless it was bespoke for such an use."

The Ascension was never "bespoke for such an use," and for years it remained in the Copley family. Today it hangs in the Museum of Fine Arts in Boston. Its levitating Christ seems heavy and a bit gross, and the gesturing hands of the Apostles and angels are awkwardly done. But as Copley's initial European work and his first original departure from portraits, it is as important in the development of his art as his *Boy with a Squirrel.* Possibly he was startled by his own daring to choose such a subject; in any event, in his next major European painting he reverted to the familiar ground of portraiture—his double likeness of Mr. and Mrs. Ralph Izard. Copley met the American couple while on a side trip to Naples to see the Raphaels, Leonardos and Titians in the collection of the King of Naples and to visit the nearby ruins of Pompeii and Herculaneum. By now steeped in classical lore, the painter amply indulged it in his portrait of the Izards, with its antique accessories and view of the Colosseum.

After seven months in Rome, Copley was ready to return to England to put what he had learned to practical use. On his way north he spent three and a half months in Parma copying Correggio's *The Holy Family with St. Jerome* on commission from an English nobleman. Copley planned to stop off in a number of other cities as well, but news from home changed his mind. In Parma he learned that full-fledged revolution had finally erupted in America and that many lives had been lost.

He may have been shocked, but he could not have been completely surprised. In his letters to Henry Pelham he had prophesied open revolt, and although he had deplored the prospect and refused to take sides he was convinced of the rebels' eventual success. Word of the outbreak produced a series of near-frantic letters from Copley to his wife, beseeching her, for safety's sake, to flee Boston immediately. "As the sword is drawn," he predicted in one letter, "all must be finally settled by the sword. I cannot think that the power of Great Britain will subdue the country, if the people are united, as they appear to be at present . . . it is very evident to

Home for Copley and his family during their first seven years in London was a house in Leicester Square—third from the right in this detail from a contemporary engraving. Other art-world notables who lived on the fashionable quadrangle were Joshua Reynolds and auctioneer James Christie. Earlier, Sir James Thornhill and the great William Hogarth had lived there.

To mark the Royal Academy's 25th anniversary in 1793, the British artist Henry Singleton painted a group portrait of the 40 Academicians in their Council chambers. West is seated and wearing a hat; Copley is leaning on a cane before a plaster cast of the Laocoön. The two Americans were no longer friends. West had been elected Academy president the year before but Copley had competed for the post—a move thought to be ungrateful, since West had been primarily responsible for Copley's admission to membership in the Academy.

me that America will have the power of resistance until grown strong to conquer, and that victory and independence will go hand in hand."

Copley's fears for his own family's security proved groundless. While still in Parma, he received news that his wife and three oldest children —Elizabeth, Mary and John Singleton Jr.—had landed in England. With them was his father-in-law, Richard Clarke. Henry Pelham was to join them later. Copley's mother, however, adamantly refused to budge from Boston, and his youngest child, a boy born after Copley's departure for Europe, had been left in her care. The baby was thought too frail to travel, and he died shortly after; his father never saw him.

Hurrying across the Continent, Copley was reunited with his family in London in October 1775, and set them up in a spacious house at 12 Leicester Square. His very choice of neighborhoods signaled the aplomb with which he launched his English career. The quarter was a fashionable one much favored by the art world. The great Reynolds lived across the square. Almost at once the enterprising Bostonian made a bid for membership in the Royal Academy, then in its seventh year. At the Academy's exhibition in 1776 Copley entered the portrait of the Izards that he had produced in Italy. It attracted no special notice, but on the strength of his earlier London success with *Boy with a Squirrel,* and fortified further by Benjamin West's efforts on his behalf, Copley was elected an Associate of the Academy, the rank just below that of Academician.

At the Academy's exhibition the following year Copley was plainly determined to make a splash. Among his entries was a portrait more complex than the Izards'—a group portrait of the artist and his family *(pages 145 and 147)* painted to celebrate their reunion. In addition to his family portrait, Copley produced likenesses of several loyalist friends who had fled America, and commissions from British sitters were also coming in. In executing them Copley began increasingly to display the free brushwork and exuberant colors that were to mark his English style of portraiture. How well he was assimilating the lessons of his new milieu is seen, for example, in the vivacious effect achieved by his brush in *Mrs. Seymour Fort (page 146);* yet at the same time the characterization of his sitter is as acute as any he achieved in Boston.

Initially, the reviews of Copley's London works were tepid, a far remove from the acclaim accorded his *Boy with a Squirrel* a decade earlier. The critic of the *Morning Chronicle,* writing of *The Copley Family* in 1777, observed that "the settee, the carpet, and the prospect through the window are so glaring that the effect of the figures is greatly destroyed, and after regarding the picture for some time it is difficult for a beholder to guess which object the painter meant to make his main subject."

The following year, however, a very different reaction occurred, and a very different kind of picture prompted it. Ever since Copley's return from Italy, and his exposure there to Renaissance masters who gloried in scenes of ancient history and mythology, he had yearned all the more to fulfill his youthful ambition to make his name as a history painter. He displayed his first effort in this direction, a commissioned work, at the Academy exhibition of 1778. But this was history painting of a startling sort. Far from hewing to the grand tradition of the old masters, Copley radically departed from it. The focus of his picture was neither a mythological character nor an ancient warrior performing some mighty deed, but an Englishman still living, shown in the throes of a terrifying experience he had had as a youth. As the catalogue for the Academy exhibition described the picture, it concerned "a boy attacked by a shark, and rescued by some seamen in a boat: founded on a fact which happened in the harbour of the Havannah." Copley's opus—the first history painting he ever produced—is now known as *Watson and the Shark (page 148).*

By the time Copley painted it, the patron who commissioned it, Brook Watson, was a prosperous London merchant of 43; later he was to become Lord Mayor of the city. The incident he asked Copley to re-create had taken place when he was 14, and swimming in the waters off Havana, Cuba. As he told the story, a shark had attacked him and bitten off his leg; the wooden leg he now proudly sported bore out his claim.

The critical applause that greeted *Watson and the Shark* was all an aspiring artist could ask. The same *Morning Chronicle* reviewer who had found fault with *The Copley Family* proclaimed the new work to be "one of the most striking pictures" at the Academy. The *St. James Chronicle* disposed of everything else in the show in one article and devoted another entirely to Copley's painting. Copley, this newspaper's critic asserted, had proved himself "a Genius who bids fair to rival the Great Masters of the Ancient Italian Schools."

What captured the critics, and the public as well, was the drama with which Copley infused his work. In it a naked Watson flounders in the water as two men strain over the side of a small boat trying to save him from the onrushing shark. Another man holds on to them, while four others row furiously. In the background the details of Havana's harbor are faithfully portrayed; the shark, however, is a chimera such as no ocean ever bred. Prints of Morro Castle and its environs were available to Copley, but not, apparently, pictures of *Carcharodon carcharias.*

As always with a nautical scene, the literal-minded found minor technical points to carp at in *Watson and the Shark*; they complained, for example, that the boat did not tip enough for the weight of the men leaning over its side, and that the rowers were handling their oars in-

When he created this family coat of arms, Brook Watson, the hero of Copley's *Watson and the Shark (page 148),* proudly included some morbid reminders of his boyhood adventure. Above the shield he placed a crest showing Neptune about to plunge his trident into a shark resembling the one that Copley depicted depriving Watson of his leg. In the shield's upper left corner is the severed limb, superimposed over a heraldic bird.

correctly. But these comments were lost in the general acclaim. Copley was never again to reap quite such praise—and honor. In February 1779 he was elected to the top rank of Royal Academician, and there can be little doubt the immense success of *Watson and the Shark* was responsible.

Almost at once Copley undertook a more ambitious history picture. This time, perhaps emboldened by his triumph, he frankly poached on territory that had been staked out by his benefactor Benjamin West. In so doing, Copley sowed the seeds of a rivalry that gradually eroded their friendship and ultimately led to open warfare between the men.

West had been acknowledged as London's leading painter of grand historical subjects ever since the sensation he made with *The Death of Wolfe (pages 126-127)* eight years earlier. Now Copley turned to another famous and dramatic death in recent British history, one linked, like Wolfe's, with events in the American colonies. The death was that of William Pitt, Earl of Chatham, who had been England's prime minister at the time of the conquest of Canada and who had remained active in politics. On April 7, 1778, in the House of Lords, Chatham sat listening as a fellow member, the Duke of Richmond, made a speech calling for George III to withdraw all British troops from the colonies and to recognize American independence. As the aged and infirm Chatham rose to protest, he collapsed, the victim of a stroke. A month later he died.

Both West and Copley conceived the idea of painting the stricken earl as he lay in the arms of his colleagues. West soon gave up his project. According to the contemporary British writer Horace Walpole, he did so in order "not to interfere with his friend Copley." At this point the two artists were still on good terms, and indeed Copley painted the magnanimous West's portrait around this time.

Copley worked for two years on *The Death of the Earl of Chatham, (pages 152-153)*, his biggest effort to date. The completed painting measured seven and a half feet high by 10 feet long and contained no fewer than 56 figures. Moreover, they were not characters of Copley's invention, like the boatmen in *Watson and the Shark,* but specific portraits of the nobles present in the House of Lords on the afternoon when Chatham collapsed. With this one canvas Copley created a new genre in art; he fused the history picture with the group portrait. Previous artists had achieved such an amalgam, but had emphasized the portraits rather than —as in Copley's painting—the historical event itself. West's *Death of Wolfe,* to be sure, balanced history and the depiction of a known personality, but the scene he chose was remote both in distance and time. Copley, on the other hand, presented a local event still fresh in popular memory, and thus gave it the powerful added impact of immediacy.

No one commissioned *The Death of Chatham;* Copley painted it entirely on speculation. But he soon displayed a bit of Yankee shrewdness. Foreseeing the picture's popularity, he decided to have a large engraving made of it and sold 2,500 advance subscriptions for the prints. To turn a further profit, he decided to exhibit the painting not at the Royal Academy, the customary showcase, but in separate quarters—for an admission fee. Copley's audacious venture, in a rented gallery in Spring Gardens and in competition with the Academy's 1781 exhibition, succeeded strikingly. In the 10 weeks the painting was on view, some 20,000 people came to see it, and attendance at the Academy show over the same period plummeted. This incident alone created much of the tension between Copley and his fellow Academicians, West included, that was to last for the rest of Copley's life. Ironically, he never found a buyer for his *Chatham;* after nearly three decades he disposed of it in a raffle.

Copley had no such difficulty selling portraits. The renown he had won with *Watson* and *Chatham* caused patrons to flock. But soon Copley's portrait style began to betray arrogance and superficiality, the curse of much 18th Century British portraiture, and these flaws were to recur more and more often during the remainder of his career.

A fellow American living in London, Elkanah Watson, also sat for a Copley portrait, and by chance was able to provide proof that the painter's home ties still tugged at him. On December 5, 1782, while the sittings were in progress, Copley and Watson suspended them to go to the House of Lords and hear George III announce that the American War of Independence was over. Copley, according to Watson, then rushed back to the portrait and "with a bold hand, a master's touch, and I believe an American heart," painted the Stars and Stripes on the flag flying from a ship in the background. "This, I imagine," Watson later wrote, "was the first American flag hoisted in England." But Copley's emotional outburst at the turn in the fortunes of his native land was evidently short-lived. He spent a good part of that year painting a subject far removed from current events: the Biblical episode of Christ, St. Peter and the imperial tax collector. He produced *The Tribute Money,* one of his rare religious works, as a belated "diploma picture" required by the membership rules of the Royal Academy.

In 1783 Copley moved his family from 12 Leicester Square to 24 George Street, where he was destined to live out his life. The neighborhood was no less fashionable, and the house, if smaller, was still elegant; moreover it had a gallery for the display of the artist's work. One on his first accomplishments in these new surroundings was *The Death of Major Peirson (pages 154-155),* a painting some Copley admirers consider his finest. Commissioned by the influential London alderman and print publisher John Boydell, Copley's latest essay in contemporary history recorded a stirring event on the British-held Channel island of Jersey in 1781—the death of the young British commander, Major Francis Peirson, at the moment of his victory over invading French troops. Like *The Death of Chatham,* this painting was not only timely but charged with realism and drama, full of flying flags, scarlet British uniforms and swirling battle smoke. And like *Chatham,* it was exhibited independently and for a fee, further annoying the Royal Academy and Copley's colleagues.

Part of the success of *Major Peirson* may have stemmed from England's need for a taste of victory after the surrender of Lord Cornwallis to General George Washington at Yorktown. The same need may have moved the Corporation of the City of London to commission a painting of *The Siege of Gibraltar,* commemorating the repulse of a Spanish fleet by the English garrison at the Rock in 1782. West was a logical candidate for the commission, but Copley's handling of the *Major Peirson* canvas had been masterful, and he was awarded the plum. The picture was to prove the largest of Copley's career—18 feet high and 25 feet long —and take him eight years to complete.

To be entrusted with this mammoth project must surely have been balm for Copley's ego, but while he was toiling at it he was dealt a blow that was to disabuse him of his standing in the British art world. In 1785 he received a commission for which he joyfully set aside *The Siege.* None other than George III himself invited Copley to paint the three youngest royal daughters, giving the artist the opportunity he had long sought to win court patronage. The portrait *(page 132)* appeared at the Academy the next year, and Copley was justified in hoping that the vivacious charm with which he had endowed the Princesses would gain him permanent royal favor. Then, however, this scornful blast appeared in the *Morning Post:* "So, Mr. Copley, is this the fruit of your long studies and labours? . . . Is it because you have heard *fine feathers* make fine birds, that you have concluded *fine cloaths* will make fine *Princesses?* What delightful disorder! Why, you have plucked up harmony by the roots, and planted confusion in its stead! Princesses, parrots, dogs, grapes, flowers, leaves, are each striving for pre-eminence, and opposing with hostile force, all attempts of our wearied eyes to find repose."

The caustic critic was John Hoppner, a fellow Academician. What motivated the unusual savagery of his attack can only be conjectured. Hoppner himself had three separate portraits of the same three Princesses in the same exhibition. Certainly Copley had not endeared himself to his colleagues by his showings away from the Academy. Perhaps most important, court patronage was tightly held by a handful of artists, Hoppner and West among them, and they did not welcome attempts to crack their monopoly. Whether George III himself agreed with Hoppner's stinging rebuke is not known, but a quarter of a century was to go by before Copley was given another chance to work for British royalty.

Another group portrait he painted, *The Sitwell Family,* fared no better than *The Three Youngest Daughters of King George III* when shown at the Royal Academy in 1787. It depicted the children of Francis Sitwell —whose descendants Edith, Osbert and Sacheverell were to become famous literary names in our own day—indulging in some genteel roughhouse in a sedate interior setting. In this work Copley stood at the crossroads between portraiture and genre, rendering the kind of scene from everyday life that was to characterize the Romantic painting of the Victorian era. But the British were not yet receptive to such works. One critic declared that the Sitwell portrait resembled "the performance of a mere Tyro in art," and others were equally uncomplimentary. Copley exhibited no more pictures at the Academy for seven years.

By 1790 he had finally finished his monumental *Siege of Gibraltar.* Once again he chose to show the work privately, this time in a huge tent in a London park. Its display coincided with the Royal Academy's 1791 exhibition and drew enormous crowds, but the critics were only lukewarm. For all its aura of heroism and some brilliant individual portraits of officers defending the Rock against the Spaniards, the painting was melodramatic and unconvincing.

Faced with the apparently implacable hostility of the people who counted in London's art circles, it is small wonder that Copley began to talk of pulling up stakes and taking his family back to Boston. But his mounting financial difficulties in London made such an expensive move impractical, if not impossible. His bid to win the lucrative patronage of the court had failed. Lawsuits with engravers of his work were draining his resources. The almost continuous 18th Century warfare between the British and the French, coupled with unrest in Britain's Irish realm, had brought on a depression in England, and even the earnings of painters more popular than Copley were being sharply curtailed. In 1795 he sold his Beacon Hill property for a good deal less than he had hoped to get for it, and thus severed his last link with Boston.

Emotionally as well as financially Copley was going through a bad time. His jealousy of his old mentor West had become almost pathological. With Reynolds' death in 1792, West had been elected president of the Royal Academy. Against what would seem to have been insuperable odds, Copley himself had aspired to the post, and thereafter feuded with his former friend over nearly every Academy issue. He was fast losing most of his other friends through his increasing truculence and touchiness, deteriorating psychologically in a way that was bound to be reflected in his works.

After the critical response to *The Siege of Gibraltar*, Copley produced several other history paintings in hopes of repeating the success of *Watson and the Shark* and *The Death of Chatham*. His efforts were in vain, and capping them was the huge and disastrous group portrait of Sir Edward Knatchbull and his family, living and dead (*pages 156-157*). Commissioned by Sir Edward in 1800 and three years in the painting, it revealed an unmistakable falling off in Copley's powers. His depiction of Knatchbull, his current wife and 10 living children was, in effect, a stiff and monotonous frieze; above them floated a ludicrous heavenly assemblage including the nobleman's two deceased wives and a pair of spirits presumed to be defunct Knatchbull offspring. Entered in the Academy exhibition of 1803, the painting provoked only laughter. Knatchbull, who had not assented to a public showing, was outraged, and succeeded in having the picture withdrawn. Coming on top of the public derision, this development must have been excruciating for Copley.

Moreover, the painting helped intensify his feud with West. Copley had won permission from the Academy's governing council to submit his canvas later than was normally allowed; in part because of its size —18 by 12 feet—and in part because of the difficulty of installing it. West, as Academy president, vetoed the council's action. Thirsting for revenge, Copley then publicized the fact that a painting by West in the same exhibition had been displayed at the Academy 27 years earlier. There was a rule against second showings, and the London newspapers accused West of deception and chicanery.

Copley's stratagem came at a time when West's own star was in decline. He no longer enjoyed the patronage of the court. The King had managed to swallow West's outspoken defense of the American Revolution, but more recently, during a truce in 1802 in the war between England

The admission ticket for Copley's exhibition of his *Siege of Gibraltar* in 1791 bore this engraving showing how the painting was displayed. Housing the huge picture had posed problems. When existing galleries proved too small, Copley set up a "magnificent Oriental tent" 84 feet long; but protests from London residents forced him to move the exhibit several times. Finally, George III invited him to use the grounds near Buckingham Palace, noting that "*My* wife won't complain." Copley later claimed 60,000 people had paid a shilling each to see the work.

and France, West had visited Paris and returned full of praise for the arch-enemy Napoleon—praise that extended even to the Corsican's "well-turned leg." This was too much for George III, and the resulting rift led to West's resignation as president of the Academy in 1805. His artist friends rallied to him, however, and in 1807 he was re-elected; he was to serve until his death in 1820 at the age of 82.

The now mortal enmity between the two American artists continued to the end. At every opportunity Copley intrigued against West in Academy affairs. West testified against Copley in a lawsuit Knatchbull brought over the high fee he had been charged for his family portrait. The quarreling diminished the prestige of both artists, but for Copley the repercussions were more damning, perhaps because the British had never warmed to him as they had to West. A colleague of both men, Joseph Farington, confided to his diary: "Copley has done more injury to the arts and the character of artists than any man of his time."

Copley produced few notable works of any kind after *The Knatchbull Family*. His old fire glowed briefly in several portraits, but most of his likenesses were pompous, expressionless, clotheshorse performances. His second and last opportunity to paint a member of the Royal Family—an equestrian portrait of the Prince of Wales *(page 159)*—had no better result; when exhibited at the Academy in 1810, the picture turned out to be a revelation of ebbing talent and desperation.

The painter from Boston was now a spent man, financially as well as artistically. For a while, after his income began to decline in the 1790s, he had borrowed from his father-in-law, Richard Clarke, who remained part of the Copley household until his death in 1795. The artist then turned to his son-in-law, Gardiner Greene, a wealthy Bostonian who married Copley's daughter Elizabeth. Still later the family was supported by Copley's son, John Jr., who became a lawyer and member of Parliament and who, as Baron Lyndhurst, was to serve as Lord High Chancellor of England under Queen Victoria. On one occasion, in his 69th year, Copley was so close to destitution that he committed an incredible crudity. Unable to obtain a private audience, he confronted George III in a corridor of the royal palace and tried to interest him in sitting for a portrait. Brusquely the King replied, "Sit to you for a portrait? What? Do you want to make a show of me?"

Despite his tribulations, Copley kept at his easel. The young artist and future inventor of the telegraph, Samuel F. B. Morse, visited him in 1811 and reported that he was "very old and infirm. . . . His powers of mind have almost entirely left him; his late paintings are miserable; it is really a lamentable thing that a man should outlive his faculties."

Like West, whose artistic gifts also disintegrated with old age, Copley lived too long for his own good. But like West, he helped initiate a new day. The agonizing drama of his *Watson and the Shark* and the warm domesticity of *The Sitwell Family* were to find echoes in the Romantic movement in art that flourished both in America and Europe during the 19th Century. In no small part, the foundations of that style were laid by the unhappy old man who, at 77, died of a stroke at his London home on September 9, 1815.

Fame and Failure

Copley landed in England from provincial Boston in 1774 eager to build a new career for himself in the more sophisticated climate of the mother country. First, he felt, he needed to absorb the lessons of the old masters at close hand, and so he set out on a 16-month pilgrimage to the shrines of classical and Renaissance art in Italy and France. Inspired and freshly confident about his future, he then settled in London to polish his style further and attract the attention of patrons and influential critics. A quick learner, Copley soon proved that he had assimilated all that he had seen of Europe's art riches.

He continued to exploit his old skills at portraiture in order to earn a living and widen his circle of acquaintances among the English upper classes. But he also began to expand his work to include larger themes. Following the path of his early mentor Benjamin West, and also partly in competition with him, Copley took on the field of historical painting. His realistic style and dramatic flair were perfectly suited to the task. Soon he captured the fancy of a large group of admirers and won election to the Royal Academy—a triumph denied many native-born English painters. In time Copley's success and the complexities of London took their toll. Perhaps he strained too hard to please his patrons or outdo his rivals; perhaps his creative powers simply ran out. Before that point, however, he produced a number of paintings that rank among the finest of the age.

Their faces almost touching, Copley's wife Sukey and son John cling in a tender embrace while his baby daughter Mary hugs her mother's arm. This charming detail from Copley's large painting *(page 147)* shows both his deep feeling for his family and the freer style he adopted after his recent exposure to Continental art.

The Copley Family, 1776-1777, detail
NATIONAL GALLERY OF ART, WASHINGTON, D.C., ANDREW MELLON FUND

Mrs. Seymour Fort, c. 177

The Copley Family, 1776-1777

Among the best of Copley's London portraits is the one at left of Mrs. Seymour Fort. Little is known about her; possibly she was the wife or widow of a successful merchant. Copley painted her with total self-assurance, presenting her as the confident, complacent Englishwoman personified. Typical of the small touches with which he lends reality to his portraits are Mrs. Fort's hands, working a shuttle and thread as she enjoys a popular pastime of the day called "knotting."

Apart from a growing mastery of technique, the portrait of Mrs. Fort gives scant hint of Copley's artistic education abroad. But in the ambitious family portrait above he seems to have drawn direct inspiration from the light and warm color of Italy. During his stay there, his family reached haven in London after fleeing the first skirmishes of the American Revolutionary War. Buoyed

by his reunion with them and by the sense of security afforded by living in England, where he felt that his art would be fully appreciated, Copley radiated optimism in the family portrait he soon completed. He himself stands in the background, holding some papers which may be symbolic of his future artistic plans. In front of him sits his father-in-law, Richard Clarke, holding little Susanna, who was to die of scarlet fever just a few years later. The beguiling child at center is another of Copley's daughters, Elizabeth, who was ultimately to marry a wealthy Bostonian and return to America. Nestling his mother is John Singleton Copley Jr., who grew up to be a distinguished solicitor and served as Lord High Chancellor under Queen Victoria. At right is the youngest Copley child, Mary, who remained with her father all his life and died a spinster in London at the age of 95.

147

Head of a Negro, 1777-1783

Copley's first historical painting in England was not, as might have been expected, a scene from classical antiquity or mythology. Rather, it concerned the grisly true experience of a 14-year-old English youth who lost his leg to a shark while swimming in Havana's harbor in 1749. The work was commissioned three decades later by the victim himself, Brook Watson, who had gone on to become a prominent merchant and still later served briefly as Lord Mayor of London.

Although hardly a major episode in history, Watson's story, as depicted by Copley, has elements of grandeur, as well as a treatment that is both original and ingenious. No other artist had ever undertaken such a theme; moreover, Copley had few details of the actual event to go by. But he charged the picture with an excitement and a reality—however theatrical—that are unique in the art of Copley's day. As the shark surges toward the naked boy, a man in the prow seeks to deflect it, while two other boatmen reach frantically for the hapless Watson. The viewer braces in suspense: Will they snatch the youth from the jaws of disaster in time?

As in the case of his subsequent large-scale English paintings, Copley made many detailed preparatory drawings for the work, and even several small oil versions, before transferring the scene to a full-size canvas. His astute study above may have served as a sketch for the black sailor in the rescue boat, a vivid reminder of Copley's expertise at capturing the subtle nuances of facial expressions.

Watson and the Shark, 1778

Midshipman Augustus Brine, 1782

The increasingly facile style of Copley's English portraits emerges in these commissioned oils of two young gentlemen of privilege. Richard Heber *(opposite),* rosy-cheeked, ruby-lipped, secure in his status as the son of a noted Anglican cleric, leans jauntily on a cricket bat while holding a ball in his left hand. If he seems unabashed by the portraitist, Augustus Brine *(above),* the son of an admiral, seems downright arrogant. His hair fashionably long, sporting crisp linens and a blue midshipman's jacket with brass buttons, he stands smartly, with a firm grip on his cocked hat. A distant storm-tossed ship and an expanse of billowing sail presage his chosen career; a massive anchor fluke directs attention to his face. Both portraits are highly accomplished; the light and shadow are strongly contrasted, the colors brilliant, the craft of the artist as confident as the boys themselves.

Richard Heber, 1782

151

Copley's fame as a history painter soared with the public showing in 1781 of *The Death of the Earl of Chatham (right)*. The picture was based on a stirring incident in the House of Lords three years earlier. The earl, a former prime minister better known to posterity as William Pitt the Elder, had risen to protest a move to recognize American independence when he was suddenly felled by a stroke; he died a month later. The intense drama of the scene in Parliament, which shocked all England, was not lost on Copley, who set out to re-create the event in paint. With characteristic attention to detail, he did not start on his large canvas until he had completed individual portraits of the 54 lords who had witnessed Pitt's collapse. He did embellish the facts, however, by clothing each man in his ceremonial robe, actually never worn during public debates.

The stricken Pitt lies amid his colleagues while his adversary, the Duke of Richmond, stands at the right, his hand extended. One of Pitt's sons clutches his father's right arm. Another foe, Lord Mansfield, remains seated at the far left; his placid, unfeeling expression is a jarring note in the general air of dismay that pervades the chamber.

Although the public acclaimed Copley's work, the picture made important enemies for him as a result of his decision to exhibit it on his own, charging admission. He thus diverted attention—and profits—from the Royal Academy exhibition where the painting would normally have been displayed.

The Death of the Earl of Chatham, 1779-1781

The Death of Major Peirson, 1783

When Copley exhibited *The Death of Major Peirson* in 1784, the chorus of praise reached all the way into Buckingham Palace. The painting was inspired by a relatively minor military incident. In 1781 French troops invading the British-owned Channel island of Jersey were routed in a counterattack led by a young Major Francis Peirson, who fell in battle just as victory was assured. The British public, smarting at defeats suffered in the American Revolutionary War, found in Peirson's heroism a comforting affirmation of the valor of the British Army, and Copley's painting reinforced it.

As in his other history paintings, Copley composed this work as if presenting a play. The action is focused squarely on center stage. The movement at the wings—soldiers charging on the left and civilians fleeing on the right—further serves to direct the eye toward the middle of the canvas. Everywhere there are supporting players: the fallen major is being avenged by a Negro servant who fires his musket into the retreating mass of enemy troops; the drummer at left ignores his own wounds to salute his dying commander. The women and children, probably modeled after Copley's own family, rush off in horror from the carnage.

Like all good melodrama, the painting is a blend of violence, agony, heroism and chaos. England's gallery goers loved it. Even before its public exhibition King George III inspected the canvas minutely and gave it his heartiest approval. Despite this royal endorsement, however, Copley never managed to secure any court commissions and was forced to rely on less august private patronage.

155

Study for Lady Knatchbull and Children, 1800-1802

Study for a Daughter (The Knatchbull Family), 1800-1802

Since portraiture was his strongest suit, Copley had reason to expect plaudits for his portrait of a country squire, Sir Edward Knatchbull, and his large family. Instead, those who saw the completed work in 1802 ridiculed it. The painting was later cut up, but the oil sketch for it *(above)* helps explain Copley's failure. Always a slow worker, he slaved over his canvas for three years. During this time, Knatchbull lost his second wife, remarried and had another child. In response to his patron's instructions, Copley included not only the second

Sketch for The Knatchbull Family, 1800-1802

wife but the first in the painting, placing them among a band of angels hovering overhead; then, at the center of the scene, he painted in the third Lady Knatchbull holding her newborn infant. As the sketches at left indicate, Copley still had a firm grasp of drawing. But his composition meanders, the subjects are deployed rather aimlessly, and the squire stands by at the right, hat tilted back, as though he had wandered into the scene mistakenly. The rejection of the portrait was a blow from which the artist never fully recovered.

157

Manfully, if somewhat pathetically, Copley struggled to regain a place of esteem in England's art world by undertaking, in 1804, an uncommissioned equestrian portrait of the Prince of Wales, later King George IV. His hopes were raised by the Prince himself. Pleased with the first sketches, he agreed to sit for Copley but kept delaying the sittings. As a result the portrait took five years to complete. Copley rested his dreams of renewed favor on the painting's reception at the Royal Academy exhibition of 1810, where it was first displayed. But once more his work was scorned; critics derided the disproportionately tiny figures in the background and the wooden stance of both the Prince and his mount. Viewed today, the portrait seems indeed a failure, but a noble one. The intent is lofty, the colors bold; in sum, however, the picture succeeds less than its few well-painted parts. Obviously, as seen in the sketches on this page of the Prince's fellow officers, Copley was losing his skill even as a draftsman; the figures lack the animation of his earlier English portraits. Years of bickering with his patrons and Academy colleagues, as well as his unsatisfied passion to win a niche in English society, seem to have drained Copley of his artistic energy. Moreover, he was now in his seventies and had been working for well over 50 years. Unwilling to quit, he spent his five remaining years in a futile effort to rekindle the brilliance of his past.

Study for George IV (as Prince of Wales),
Lord Heathfield, 1804-1806

Study for George IV (as Prince of Wales), 1804-1809

George IV (as Prince of Wales), 1804-1809

159

VII

The New Generation

John Singleton Copley and Benjamin West had left America convinced that only by steeping themselves in Europe's great art traditions could they find artistic fulfillment. They never returned, but many of the American artists who rose to prominence after the War of Independence and during the early 19th Century were beholden to Copley and West for inspiration or personal guidance or both. The major painters of this new galaxy differed from their expatriate predecessors in one highly significant way. John Trumbull, Charles Willson Peale, Gilbert Stuart and Samuel F. B. Morse also traveled abroad to absorb the lessons of classical and Renaissance art. But unlike Copley and West these men came home. They were on hand to record all the ambience of the fledgling American republic—its history, its leaders, its natural beauty, its interests and its promise. Whatever they owed to the heritage of Europe, they endowed their own works with a peculiarly American flavor.

Trumbull, one of the first to emerge of the new generation of painters, was almost totally blind in one eye as a result of a childhood accident. That he chose to disregard this obstacle was perhaps in itself peculiarly American. He decided to become an artist, he later recalled, when at the age of 15 he chanced to visit Copley at his home on Boston's Beacon Hill and saw paintings that were "the first I had ever seen deserving the name." Trumbull, the precocious and self-centered son of the governor of the Connecticut colony, was then a student at Harvard. He proceeded to spend his spare time after classes making copies—both drawings and oils—of works by Copley and various Europeans. After his graduation in 1773 and a two-year stint in the Revolutionary army he resumed painting and produced some portraits that clearly show his debt to Copley.

When he was 24 Trumbull sailed for England, eager to improve his style. The year was 1780 and the Revolutionary War still raged, but British authorities in Boston assured Trumbull that he would be allowed entry into their country. In London, however, he was seized almost immediately. News had just arrived of the Americans' execution of the British Major John André for having conspired with the traitorous Benedict Arnold to hand West Point over to the British commander in New

In his mid-forties and grown wise in the ways of his adopted London, Copley sat for this portrait by a young fellow American, Gilbert Stuart, then on the rise as a fashionable portraitist in the English capital. An extremely facile craftsman, Stuart often poked fun at Copley's slow, methodical work habits, but his study of his older colleague bespeaks a basic respect.

Gilbert Stuart: *John Singleton Copley*, c. 1783-1784

York. In retaliation Trumbull was imprisoned. Seven months later he was freed on condition that he leave England, and he passed the remainder of the war traveling on the Continent.

With the peace he returned to London and joined West's studio. West's enthusiasm for history painting was contagious, for Trumbull ambitiously decided to paint a series of works based on the late war. Both his *Death of General Montgomery* and his *Bunker's Hill (pages 180-181),* an event he himself had observed from a nearby vantage point during his soldier days, were painted in West's studio. Considering their grand subject matter, they were unusually small in size, only three by two feet. West had urged this idea, feeling that Trumbull's damaged sight might cause him to distort a larger picture. Each painting, with its dying hero supported in the arms of his men, was plainly modeled after West's *Death of Wolfe (pages 126-127).*

Over the next two decades Trumbull traveled a great deal between Europe and America. He was a man of many tastes, incapable of concentrating solely on art. In the 1790s he made a number of forays into revolution-torn France to buy old masters from hard-pressed aristocrats for resale in England at a profit. His American passport also proved handy when war erupted between Britain and France; he was able to buy French brandy on behalf of English entrepreneurs. But a swamped vessel that badly soaked a load of old masters, and a beached brandy boat, finally convinced Trumbull that his fortune lay in his original career. In 1804, when he was 48, he returned to America and set up as a portraitist in New York.

The era of his greatest fame began in 1816, with the award of a prestigious commission he had long sought: to paint four large murals for the Rotunda of the new Capitol building in Washington. Trumbull achieved this coup through the intercession of an old acquaintance and admirer, Thomas Jefferson, by then living in retirement at Monticello. The murals he produced are greatly enlarged versions of four works in the historical series he had launched three decades earlier in West's studio in London: *Declaration of Independence, The Surrender of General Burgoyne, The Surrender of Lord Cornwallis* and *The Resignation of General Washington.* In size they average about 18 by 12 feet, some six times larger than the original canvases. But while the small paintings are compact and clear, the murals are overblown and distorted. When Trumbull completed them he was more than 60, a tired man past his prime, whose weakened sight was an added handicap.

Whether Trumbull's talents might have flourished more strikingly in a field other than history painting is an intriguing question. In his last years he produced a series of small, appealing landscapes. They prophesy the interest in that genre that would preoccupy subsequent American painters such as Frederick Church, Thomas Cole and Winslow Homer. Thus, in a sense, Trumbull heralded not only a new turn in American art but a new tendency in the American character: the growing assertion of pride in a bountiful land and its natural beauties—and wonders. Several of Trumbull's landscapes, for example, extol the drama of Niagara Falls, a subject that would captivate a parade of painters in years to come.

Matthew Pratt's *The American School* depicts the London studio of Benjamin West, who devoted hours every morning to instructing fellow artists. Many American painters—including John Trumbull, Gilbert Stuart, Copley and Pratt himself—received tutelage from their famous compatriot, but the identity of the artists in this painting is unknown. West himself, however, is believed to be the standing figure at left.

Only one other American phenomenon so engrossed the native artist: George Washington. Of all those who portrayed him, however, one —Gilbert Stuart—is pre-eminent. To most Americans, in fact, the name of Stuart means but one thing, the bust portrait of Washington that hangs in countless schoolrooms, public buildings and places of honor. Actually, Stuart did much more with Washington than this single study. He is believed to have painted about 110 portraits of the great man, and hundreds more have been falsely attributed to him.

The linkage of Washington and Stuart has its special irony. The indelible image we now have of the Father of Our Country, austere and impeccably correct, was fashioned by a painter whose own life was an orgy of excesses. Stuart's chronic irresponsibility with money kept him constantly under threat of imprisonment for debt. A big, sloppy man, he regularly ate and drank with an abandon most men reserve for holiday feasts. Another of his notable addictions was snuff, which he inhaled into his bulbous nose from a snuffbox "nearly as large round as the top of a small hat." He excused this failing by claiming that it was not his fault, he had been born in a snuff mill. And, like most of Stuart's blunt statements about himself, this was the truth. His father was a snuff grinder, an improvident Scotsman, also named Gilbert, who had settled in Kingston, Rhode Island, where Stuart was born in 1755.

Raised in poverty, he picked up portrait painting as an apprentice to an itinerant Scottish artist with whom he wandered through the colonies drumming up commissions. At the first rumbles of the Revolution Stuart sailed for London. War was not to his fancy and he had no political allegiances. In the English capital his painting ability impressed West, and he served as chief apprentice in West's studio for five years. They made an odd pair: West, the sober creator of broad historical canvases; Stuart, the rakish observer of human nature, ever more confident in his gift for painting faces. Stuart loved to tease West about his preference in subject matter, asserting that "no one would paint history who could do a portrait."

Stuart himself was destined to practice within the narrowest range of any of America's second generation of painters. He was solely a portraitist; moreover, he specialized in the face; moreover, his main interest was flesh tone. The very thought of it caused him to rhapsodize. Flesh, he declared, "is like no other substance under heaven. It has all the gaiety of a silk-mercer's shop without its gaudiness and gloss, and all the soberness of old mahogany without its sadness." Flesh was the focus of Stuart's portraits; every color on the canvas was keyed to its tone. In his obsession with the human complexion—critics derided it as his "milk and rosewater" style—he sometimes neglected to fill in the costume details or setting of a portrait. As a result some of his paintings look "unfinished." But so far as he was concerned, a portrait was complete once the face was executed to his liking.

Stuart emerged from West's studio with a highly luminous, cosmopolitan style reminiscent of the ranking English portraitists of the day —Reynolds, Romney and, particularly, Gainsborough. His first big success, *The Skater (page 174)*, was not only compared favorably with

Gainsborough's work but was often in later years attributed to the Englishman. *The Skater,* which appeared at the Royal Academy exhibition of 1782, made Stuart the talk of London's art world. Reviewers cheered both its originality and its high style. Stuart opened his own studio and portrait commissions poured in.

His brush, however, could not keep pace with his tastes in living. In 1787, without telling any of his friends, he disappeared from London with his wife, a beautiful English girl whom he had married in 1786, and their small son and daughter. (Among the unpaid debts he left behind was a snuff bill of £80.) The Stuarts surfaced in Dublin, where an incisive portrait of the Lord Chancellor of Ireland, John Fitzgibbon *(page 175),* served as the painter's introduction to local connoisseurs. But as in London, his creditors outnumbered his patrons. In 1793, when he was 37, he sailed for home and for new renown in New York, Philadelphia and Boston as America's portrait painter supreme.

Admiring sitters discovered that he had a notable knack for small talk. His ability to chat endlessly on all manner of subjects was, of course, extremely useful: he could distract a sitter from a stiff pose or find in some animated reply the key to the subject's personality. Just once did this talent fail him—when the President of the United States finally agreed to sit for him in September 1795.

Washington's attitude toward portraitists was charitable, and he accommodated as many as possible. But the rigors of posing are clearly reflected in the expression he wears in their works. When Stuart first studied his famous subject his heart fell. "An apathy seemed to seize him," he wrote, "and a vacuity spread over his countenance most appalling to paint." As an opening gambit, Stuart remarked, "Now, Sir, you must let me forget that you are General Washington and that I am Stuart the painter." With his natural formality Washington responded: "Mr. Stuart need never feel the need of forgetting who he is, or who General Washington is." Repeated attempts at small talk proved futile.

The portrait was duly completed and attracted much favorable comment when it was displayed in Philadelphia, then the young nation's capital. But Stuart was unhappy with his work. He knew that he had neither discovered nor revealed the real Washington. This first effort shows the right side of Washington's face, his shoulders enormous as they crowd against the frame. One of the three basic versions in which Stuart painted Washington, it is now known as the Vaughan type, for Samuel Vaughan, an American who lived in London and who owned the portrait for years. Stuart, perennially desperate for money, made some 15 copies of the original and sold them all at a good price.

His next study of Washington used the bust portrait as a model for the face but showed the figure full length. This work is called the Lansdowne after a Pennsylvania estate where it hung for years. Stuart was dissatisfied with this painting, too, but in 1796 had yet another chance at the President, under the most propitious of circumstances: the new portrait was commissioned by Martha Washington herself.

The sittings took place at Stuart's studio, a stone barn in Germantown, outside Philadelphia. Initially, the President wore his customary bleak ex-

This Gilbert Stuart portrait of Washington, the most familiar image in American art, was copied more than 70 times by the artist himself and countlessly by others; one shrewd merchant even commissioned a batch of cheap imitations to be made in China, a piracy Stuart countered with a lawsuit. Stuart was especially pleased with this portrait because in it he was able to bring out Washington's humanity, a quality he was aided in capturing because the President was wearing a more comfortable new set of false teeth when he posed.

pression. At one point, however, he abruptly perked up when he saw a fine thoroughbred horse gallop by the window. Stuart caught the flash of interest and immediately began to talk about local horse racing. Washington's face became animated, and soon sitter and painter were chatting amiably. Meanwhile, Stuart's brush worked quickly to capture his subject's forceful personality and human side.

The result is the portrait familiar to every American. The most popular representation of Washington of the time, it is known today as the Athenaeum portrait, after the Boston Athenaeum, which owns it. Ironically, Stuart never gave the painting to Mrs. Washington. He kept it all his life, even though Washington himself came to the studio to demand it. Eventually, the Washingtons received a copy. Stuart, recognizing a money-maker when he saw one, made at least 70 copies. He called them his "hundred-dollar bills," the price per copy he sold them for when he needed quick cash. In time Stuart made a more lasting dent on American currency. His memorable third Washington portrait served as the model for the likeness perpetuated on our dollar bill.

Thishappy juncture of art and public service was not Stuart's triumph alone. The images of Franklin, Jefferson and Madison seen on our paper currency, coinage and postage stamps are all based on portraits from life by another remarkably gifted painter, an older contemporary of Stuart's, Charles Willson Peale. A personal friend of most of the Founding Fathers, Peale seems to have been acutely aware that he was preserving the features of his famous subjects for future generations. His portraits are penetrating yet more formal, more polished than Stuart's. He, too, painted Washington—and much more to Washington's satisfaction.

Peale was born near Annapolis in 1741. His mother was a seamstress, his father a schoolteacher who had fled his native England to avoid prosecution for embezzlement. The family had neither status nor money, and Peale was apprenticed to a saddle maker when he was 12. By the time he was 20 he had his own harness shop. But he soon displayed the restless, boundless energy that was to distinguish him all his life. Unsatisfied with his lot, he took up painting, having read in a book on the manual trades the quaint assertion that in painting there was good money to be made with little labor. For a time he painted shop signs and portraits between saddle-making jobs, but his debts piled up, both his trades suffered, and he decided to put some distance between himself and his creditors, fleeing north to Boston. Copley was then near the peak of his American fame, and for some months Peale hung about Copley's studio, painting portraits and miniatures and picking up technical help. On his return home he announced himself as a professional portraitist, devoted exclusively to his new career.

He became so good at it so quickly that in 1767 a group of Maryland gentlemen financed a trip to London for him to survey the masters in his field. Inevitably he ended up studying with West—about a decade before Stuart joined the studio. Peale remained in London for two years, showing his mettle as a colonial by refusing to doff his hat when George III's carriage passed by. He was better disposed toward England's fashionable portrait style, and readily absorbed its essentials. Soon after he re-

Washington appears as commander in chief of the Continental army in Charles Willson Peale's 1779 portrait. The painting commemorates the American victories at Trenton and Princeton in 1777. Peale himself was a militia captain in both battles, and he knowledgeably included a captured Hessian flag *(right)* and Princeton's Nassau Hall *(background)* as symbols of triumph. Washington hated to pose for portraits, but he granted his friend and fellow soldier Peale 14 sittings over a 23-year period.

turned to Maryland his services began to be sought out by influential patrons, and he was on his way to fame.

Before long he was as much a celebrity as many of the men he painted. John Adams, who met Peale in Philadelphia in 1776, found him interesting and important enough to record in some detail the impression the painter made: "A tender, soft, affectionate creature. . . . He is ingenious. He has vanity, loves finery, wears a sword, gold lace, speaks French, is capable of friendship and strong family attachments and natural affections."

There was much more Adams could have added, for Peale was also one of the most engaging and productive Americans of all time. Increasingly it became plain that art was not his only forte. He was also a humanist, a student of "natural philosophy" and an inventor.

Peale's most enduring contribution to science, however, was the founding of America's first great museum of natural history. In 1784 a friend presented him with a popular curiosity of the time, a stuffed paddlefish, so called because of its long paddlelike snout. Peale's own insatiable curiosity extended to all the creatures of the world, and he was so enchanted with his gift that he put it on exhibit in his picture gallery in Philadelphia, where he then lived. Within three years Peale had turned his studio into a museum.

When these quarters proved too small to house a steadily growing collection of stuffed fish, birds and assorted animals, the museum was moved to no less a place than the second floor of Independence Hall, which Peale, with typical enterprise, acquired rent free from the State Legislature. Peale's fertile mind also solved the problem of presenting his acquisitions properly. He invented the habitat group—the display of birds and animals in natural poses against painted backdrops that resembled their normal abodes.

For all the sensational success of his museum, it would never have occurred to Peale to relinquish his paints and brushes. Art retained its hold on him throughout his life. Sometimes he wedded it to his interest in science by painting backdrops for his habitat groups; on one occasion he produced a large oil of his adventures in excavating a mastodon *(pages 172-173)*. Peale also painted a portrait of his own family *(pages 170-171)*, and it is a work of more than perfunctory interest, for Peale's family was to prove another of his very special achievements. His brood was still small when he painted it as a young father, and the wife he portrayed was only his first. Over the years he was left a widower three times and he was vigorously courting a potential fourth wife when he died at 86. In all, Peale fathered 17 sons and daughters. With his usual aplomb he named most of them after artists or scientists—among others, Raphaelle, Rembrandt, Rubens, Titian, Angelica Kauffmann, Linnaeus and Franklin. Son Rembrandt won his own fame as a portraitist and son Raphaelle was America's first important specialist in still lifes. Some of the progeny of Peale's brother James, whom he had trained as a painter, also became artists. And so no small part of Peale's legacy was the most impressive dynasty in the annals of art.

Peale's own virtuoso performance would have been hard to match,

One of Charles Willson Peale's many inventions was this portable polygraph, from which he expected quick commercial success. The device could be equipped with two or more arms, each holding a pen. As the writer moved one pen, the others moved in unison, making copies of a drawing or a document on separate pieces of paper. Peale won many friends for his polygraph, including Thomas Jefferson. But its delicate machinery often jammed; this hampered its effectiveness and limited its sale. Among other inventions Peale conceived were an apple-peeling machine, a portable steam bath, and a set of dentures for George Washington made of elk's teeth mounted in lead.

but in an era when art and science had not yet gone their separate ways a younger man from Massachusetts also put on a remarkable display of versatility. Unlike Peale, Samuel Finley Breese Morse was not entirely happy about the wide-ranging nature of his gifts. He wanted desperately to make his name as a great painter, but he is remembered chiefly as the inventor of the telegraph. By the time he had perfected his notion that electric signals might be sent over wire and was ready to telegraph his now-historic words, "What hath God wrought?" as the first message so sent, the world had largely forgotten what Morse had wrought in art.

He was born across the Charles River from Boston in Charlestown in 1791, the son of a minister who was also a geographer. An interest in science came naturally and was whetted during Morse's student days at Yale when he heard some lectures on the mysterious, newly discovered "fluid" called electricity. But painting had a stronger pull for him and in 1811 he went to London to study with West. Morse had already decided that he liked history painting and disliked portraiture, and West predictably encouraged this bias. But the only market Morse found when he returned to America was in portraits. After more than a decade, however, Morse tired of his work, and was also disconsolate over the death of his wife. He decided to return to Europe; friends financed his way by giving him commissions both for original paintings and copies of old masters. But once in Paris he hit upon an idea that was to result in a landmark in American art history.

Morse was fascinated by the Louvre. Originally it had been a royal palace, but Napoleon had converted it into a national museum in 1794, filling it with the loot of his conquests, a fabulous treasure of Western art. The masterpieces on display had served countless artists as textbooks, but few ordinary citizens had seen them, and still fewer Americans. Walking the halls of the Louvre entranced, Morse conceived an ambitious scheme. He resolved to paint a view of the great Salon Carré, its walls covered with pictures, to take his painting back to America and to put it on public exhibition for a fee; thus, he reasoned, American viewers could have a tour of the Louvre without ever leaving home. The concept was, to say the least, audacious.

Morse brought the picture *(pages 178-179)* back to America as planned and exhibited it in New York, expecting next to take it on tour in other cities and towns. But public interest was scant and paid admissions were few. Morse's grand dream faded, and ultimately he sold his huge canvas —nine feet wide and some six feet high—to finance his work on the telegraph. He got only $1,200 for *The Louvre,* less than half the price he asked. Subsequently, although he held a position as professor of painting and sculpture at New York University, he devoted most of his time and energy to his scientific interests. His brushes and palette gathered dust.

Despite his failure to excite the American public with *The Louvre,* by painting it Morse unknowingly wrote a Declaration of Independence for American artists. Demonstrating an unabashed self-confidence by copying a galleryful of European old masters, he placed himself on an equal footing with them, and thus—for himself and his fellows—ended an era that began with Copley's dreams of Old World elegance.

From this cumbersome wooden prototype, Samuel F. B. Morse eventually developed the modern rapid-relay telegraph. On this primitive model the messages were not sent by an audible code of dots and dashes and there was no signal key. Instead, a stick set with metal slugs, each with distinctive ridges representing a letter, was cranked through the sending device *(foreground)*. The slugs caused a circuit breaker to rise and fall, creating electrical impulses that activated a stylus hanging from a pendulumlike frame in the receiving end *(background)*. The stylus swung back and forth on a paper tape, leaving a series of saw-tooth marks that corresponded to the ridges on the slugs. This jagged line could then be decoded by the person at the receiving end.

Four Who Came Home

Following in the footsteps of Copley and West, many younger colonial painters also traveled to Europe to see and absorb its art. Four of the best—Charles Willson Peale, John Trumbull, Gilbert Stuart and Samuel F. B. Morse—studied under West himself. But unlike their predecessors they chose to come home, determined to apply the artistic lessons of the Old World in the New and to make their fortunes in the process. The America they returned to, however, had little time to appreciate —or money to buy—their works. Its struggles for independence preoccupied the young nation: its energies were directed toward sustaining a viable government, reviving trade and taming the frontier.

And so disappointment beset the returning artists. They found some market for portraits, but not for the more ambitious canvases they envisioned, and they sought other outlets for their vitality. Only Stuart kept single-mindedly—and successfully—at his easel. Peale opened a museum of natural history in Philadelphia *(right)*. Morse switched from art to invention. Trumbull's frustrations drove him back to Europe several times, where he dabbled in such diverse pursuits as art dealing and French-brandy importing. But despite forays into other fields, these were the men who, by picturing the new nation's people and deeds, put American art on its feet. Indeed, their restless creativity helped establish a broad base for America's cultural advance.

Welcoming the viewer to his museum, the multitalented Charles Willson Peale raises a plush curtain in this self-portrait painted near the end of his long and colorful career. The museum, opened in 1786, was the first of its kind in the colonies. Its exhibits ranged from stuffed birds to the fossil bones of a mastodon, partially seen at right, that Peale himself dug up in 1801.

Charles Willson Peale: *The Artist in His Museum*, 1822

Charles Willson Peale: *The Staircase Group,* c. 1795

Charles Willson Peale: *The Peale Family,* 1809

Peale was an artist of skill, wit and gusto. Trained as a saddle maker, he was moved to paint after seeing some canvases in Virginia. He is believed to have worked briefly with Copley in Boston, joined West's London studio in 1767, and on his return to America two years later earned his living as an itinerant portraitist.

Peale had a large, close-knit family, which he memorialized in the painting above. The theme is a drawing lesson. Peale's brother St. George sits at left, sketching his mother at the far right. Next to him brother James looks on, smiling. Above them the painter himself, palette and brushes in hand, offers encouragement. One sister leans on his shoulder; another sits beside her mother, who holds one of Peale's daughters. His first of three wives, Rachel, sits at center, with another daughter.

Standing at right is the prim-faced family nurse near three classical busts sculpted by Peale.

The artist had 17 children in all—nine boys and eight girls—most of whom he named after and trained to be either painters or scientists. He portrayed two of his sons, Titian and Raphaelle, in a *trompe l'oeil* picture *(left)* that reveals his flair both for realism and for whimsy. Peale painted it when he was 54, as proof to his colleagues that his talents had not waned. Titian peers down the stairs, while Raphaelle ascends them. To heighten the realistic effect of the work, Peale hung the picture in an unused doorway of his museum and added an actual wooden step at the bottom of the canvas. So convincing was the result that when a family friend, George Washington, first saw the painting he greeted the boys with a nod.

Charles Willson Peale; *Exhuming the Mastodon*, 1806-1808

A s time went on, Peale became more and more engrossed in scientific study and collecting. Beginning with items like Benjamin Franklin's dead cat, the museum's collection gradually grew to include more exotic treasures. Always on the lookout for possible additions, Peale rushed to upstate New York in 1801 when he learned that a farmer near Newburgh had discovered the bones of a huge and obviously extinct animal in a swampy pit. On the spot he paid the farmer $300 for the bones and the right to excavate further. With equipment borrowed from the Army and Navy, Peale eagerly launched the first extensive archeological dig in America. About seven years after he finished, he commemorated the project with the painting at left. Long out of practice, Peale feared making a "daub of it," and toiled over the canvas for at least two years.

Along with its recording of early archeological techniques, the scene served Peale as an excuse for a family reunion. Various Peale children, relatives and friends appear regardless of whether they had been at the site or not. Peale himself is seen as the neatly dressed impresario at the right holding one end of a scale drawing of the excavated beast's leg. Behind him is his third wife, Hannah. Sons Rembrandt and Rubens stand by the drawing while its other end is held by Raphaelle.

The giant wheel at the center is a treadmill powered by human volunteers and used to remove water from the excavation. Near the wheel, to the right, two of Peale's younger sons, Linnaeus and Franklin, grasp a pole that leads to a floating cylinder. Standing alone, at the left, with arms folded, is the famed ornithologist Alexander Wilson, a close friend of Peale's. The owner of the land, John Masten, climbs a ladder in the foreground.

The digging unearthed the bones of two mastodons, great elephantlike prehistoric mammals. But since little was known about the beast at the time, Peale dubbed his find "The Great American Incognitum."

Gilbert Stuart developed his sophisticated portrait style under West's tutelage in London. Spirited and gregarious, Stuart had a knack for chatting genially with his sitters whatever their social rank, setting them at ease and then portraying them with elegance but candor. The story behind *The Skater (right)* illustrates his approach. When the subject, a gentleman named William Grant, arrived for his first sitting, the day happened to be a wintry one, and the relaxed small talk logically turned to skating. Soon both artist and patron were out gliding on the Serpentine, a man-made lake in London's Hyde Park. When the sitting resumed, Stuart was inspired to paint Grant as a skater. And when the portrait appeared at the Royal Academy exhibition of 1782, its originality secured Stuart's reputation.

Although besieged by lucrative commissions, Stuart lived beyond his means, and in 1787 had to flee to Dublin to escape his creditors. There he was befriended by John Fitzgibbon, Lord Chancellor and virtual dictator of Ireland. In Stuart's unflinching portrait *(far right),* Fitzgibbon's haughty face and stance epitomize the man of power.

Gilbert Stuart: *The Skater,*

174

Gilbert Stuart: *John, Lord Fitzgibbon,* 1789

After his return to America in 1792, Stuart soon demonstrated his expertise with his study *(right)* of Mrs. Richard Yates of New York. Old but sharp, she is captured at a single moment in time, her eyes seeming to appraise a sudden visitor, her busy hands arrested in their task. The work is reminiscent of Copley's *Mrs. Seymour Fort (page 146),* and proves that, like Copley, Stuart can be ranked with Europe's finest portraitists.

His study of the woman above is softer and more emotional, and with good reason. Stuart's marriage was in shambles because of his heavy drinking and high living, and he found both solace and inspiration in the beautiful Mrs. Perez Morton of Boston, wife of a lawyer and herself a poetess of merit. Her portrait by Stuart eloquently reveals his infatuation and his talent for catching the nuances of the human personality.

Gilbert Stuart: *Mrs. Richard Yates*, c. 1793

177

Samuel F. B. Morse: *Exhibition Gallery of the Louvre*, 1832-1833

Posterity remembers Samuel F. B. Morse primarily as inventor of the telegraph, but he spent much of his life toiling for recognition as a painter. His early talent for art led his father, a stern New England minister, to send him to London in 1811 to study under West. There Morse acquired a passion for painting sweeping sagas of mythological and historical events. Once home again, however, he could earn a living only by making portraits. Unhappy at this outcome, he returned to Europe in 1829, when he was 38, and in Paris he executed a painting that for sheer bravado and self-confidence is unsurpassed in the annals of 19th Century American art.

The work shows the interior of the famous Salon Carré of the Louvre, in which Morse has copied an array of the museum's masterpieces by Leonardo, Titian, Raphael, Rubens, Van Dyck and other titans. To give the painting balance and harmony, Morse has strategically placed several visitors and copyists in the foreground. At the center he shows a man, perhaps Morse himself, pointing an instructive finger, leaning over the shoulder of a female copyist. If this is indeed Morse, planted symbolically in the middle of a treasury of the greatest Western art, he seems to be confidently announcing his own place in it, as if to say American art has come of age.

On his return to America, Morse worked on portrait commissions and landscapes and longed in vain for a government commission to decorate the Capitol in Washington. But his art was taken for granted, and eventually he became preoccupied with science and photography. Some qualms persisted. In 1849 Morse wrote to his friend James Fenimore Cooper, "Alas, the very name of *picture* produces a sadness of heart I cannot describe. Painting has been a smiling mistress to many, but she has been a cruel jilt to me; I did not abandon her, she abandoned me."

179

180

John Trumbull: *Declaration of Independence,* 1786 to before 1797

John Trumbull: *Battle of Bunker's Hill,* 1786

John Trumbull is celebrated as the artist of the American Revolution. He began a series of 12 paintings on the subject, audaciously enough, while in London studying with West in 1784. One of the first and best of Trumbull's series is *Battle of Bunker's Hill (left).* The scene is charged with the romance of war; the British surge up the hill, the embattled militiamen hold firm, musket smoke hangs heavy in the air. The figure on the ground is the Revolutionary leader Major General Joseph Warren; already severely wounded, he is being attacked with a bayonet while an aide desperately fends off the thrust with his bare hand. By contrast, Trumbull's *Declaration of Independence (above)* is much less dramatic; in fact the American statesman John Randolph derided it as "the shin piece" because of the many legs that crowd the bottom of the painting. The spirit of the work, however, comes through in the careful characterizations. In particular, the faces of five men—John Adams, Roger Sherman, Robert Livingston, Thomas Jefferson and Benjamin Franklin *(detail, overleaf)*—show how well Trumbull captured the solemnity of the occasion and the humanity of the signers. In 1817 the artist was commissioned to make replicas of four scenes from his series for the Rotunda of the newly completed Capitol in Washington. They endure today as a testament, not only to Trumbull, but to America's pioneer painters.

APPENDIX

Chronology: Artists of Copley's Era

1700	1775	1850

UNITED STATES

JOHN SMIBERT   1688-1751

PETER PELHAM   c. 1695-1751

JOSEPH BLACKBURN   c. 1700-1763

ROBERT FEKE   c. 1705-c. 1750

JOSEPH BADGER   1708-1765

JOHN GREENWOOD   1727-1792

MATTHEW PRATT   1734-1805

JOHN WOLLASTON   fl. 1736-1767

JOHN SINGLETON COPLEY   1738-1815

BENJAMIN WEST   1738-1820

CHARLES WILLSON PEALE   1741-1827

WINTHROP CHANDLER   1747-1790

RALPH EARL   1751-1801

JOSEPH STEWARD   1753-1822

GILBERT STUART   1755-1828

JOHN TRUMBULL   1756-1843

REUBEN MOULTHROP   1763-1814

JOHN DURAND   fl. 1766-1782

RICHARD JENNYS   fl. 1770-1800

RAPHAELLE PEALE   1774-1825

JOHN VANDERLYN   1775-1852

REMBRANDT PEALE   1778-1860

WASHINGTON ALLSTON   1779-1843

EDWARD HICKS   1780-1849

WILLIAM JENNYS   fl. 1790-1802

SAMUEL F. B. MORSE   1791-1872

FRANCIS WILLIAM EDMONDS   1806-1863

WILLIAM SIDNEY MOUNT   1807-1868

D. G. STOUTER   fl. 1840

WAGGUNO   fl. 1858

FRANCE

FRANÇOIS BOUCHER   1703-1770

JEAN-BAPTISTE GREUZE   1725-1805

JEAN-HONORÉ FRAGONARD   1732-1806

JACQUES-LOUIS DAVID   1748-1825

ENGLAND

WILLIAM HOGARTH   1697-1764

RICHARD WILSON   1714-1782

EDWARD PENNY   1714-1791

JOHN BOYDELL   1719-1804

JOSHUA REYNOLDS   1723-1792

GAVIN HAMILTON (SCOTTISH)   1723-1798

THOMAS GAINSBOROUGH   1727-1788

JOSEPH WRIGHT (OF DERBY)   1734-1797

GEORGE ROMNEY   1734-1802

NATHANIEL DANCE   1735-1811

WILLIAM WILLIAMS   fl. 1746-1747

FRANCIS WHEATLEY   1747-1801

JOSEPH FARINGTON   1747-1821

HENRY RAEBURN   1756-1823

THOMAS ROWLANDSON   1756-1827

WILLIAM BLAKE   1757-1827

JOHN HOPPNER   1758-1810

JOHN OPIE   1761-1807

GEORGE MORLAND   1763-1804

JOHN CROME   1768-1821

THOMAS LAWRENCE   1769-1830

THOMAS GIRTIN   1775-1802

J. M. W. TURNER   1775-1851

JOHN CONSTABLE   1776-1837

JOHN SELL COTMAN   1782-1842

DAVID WILKIE   1785-1841

BENJAMIN ROBERT HAYDON   1786-1846

GERMANY

ANTON MENGS   1728-1779

SWITZERLAND

JEAN-ÉTIENNE LIOTARD   1702-1789

ANGELICA KAUFFMANN   1740-1807

HENRY FUSELI (JEAN-HENRI FÜSSLI)   1741-1825

SPAIN

FRANCISCO GOYA Y LUCIENTES   1746-1828

1700	1775	1850

Copley's predecessors, contemporaries and successors are grouped here in chronological order according to country. The bands correspond to the life spans of the artists or, where this information is unknown, to the approximate periods when they flourished (indicated by the abbreviation "fl.").

Bibliography

*Available in paperback

COPLEY—HIS LIFE AND WORK

Amory, Martha Babcock, *The Domestic and Artistic Life of John Singleton Copley, R.A.* Houghton Mifflin Company, 1882.

Flexner, James Thomas, *John Singleton Copley.* Houghton Mifflin Company, The Riverside Press, 1948.

Letters and Papers of John Singleton Copley and Henry Pelham, 1739-1776, Guernsey Jones, ed. Vol. LXXI, Massachusetts Historical Society Collections, 1914.

Parker, Barbara Neville, and Ann Bolling Wheeler, *John Singleton Copley: American Portraits in Oil, Pastel and Miniature with Biographical Sketches.* Massachusetts Museum of Fine Arts, 1938.

Prown, Jules David, *John Singleton Copley.* 2 vols. Harvard University Press, 1966.

OTHER AMERICAN ARTISTS

Burroughs, Alan, *John Greenwood in America.* Addison Gallery of American Art, 1943.

Evans, Grose, *Benjamin West and the Taste of His Times.* Southern Illinois University Press, 1959.

Flexner, James Thomas, *Gilbert Stuart.* Alfred A. Knopf, 1955.

Foote, Henry Wilder, *John Smibert, Painter.* Harvard University Press, 1950.

Galt, John, *The Life of Benjamin West.* Scholars' Facsimiles & Reprints, 1960.

Mount, Charles Merrill, *Gilbert Stuart: A Biography.* W. W. Norton & Company, Inc., 1964.

Sellers, Charles Coleman:
The Artist of the Revolution: The Early Life of Charles Willson Peale. Feather and Good Publishers, 1939.
Charles Willson Peale. 2 vols. The American Philosophical Society, 1947.

ART—HISTORICAL AND CULTURAL BACKGROUND

Alden, John R., *The American Revolution.* Harper & Brothers, 1954.

Black, Mary, and Jean Lipman, *American Folk Painting.* Clarkson N. Potter, Inc., 1966.

Burroughs, Alan, *Limners and Likenesses: Three Centuries of American Painting.* Harvard University Press, 1936.

Dunlap, William, *History of the Rise and Progress of the Arts of Design in the United States.* 3 vols. Bayley-Goodspeed, 1918.

Eliot, Alexander, *Three Hundred Years of American Painting.* Random House, 1957.

Flexner, James Thomas:
America's Old Masters, rev. ed.* Dover Publications, 1967.
Light of Distant Skies. Harcourt, Brace and Company, 1954.

Forbes, Esther, *Paul Revere and the World He Lived In.* Houghton Mifflin Company, 1942.

Green, Samuel M., *American Art.* Ronald Press, 1966.

Hagen, Oskar, *The Birth of the American Tradition in Art.* Charles Scribner's Sons, 1940.

Isham, Samuel, *The History of American Painting.* The Macmillan Company, 1927.

Larkin, Oliver W., *Art and Life in America,* rev. ed. Holt, Rinehart and Winston, 1960.

McLanathan, Richard, *The American Tradition in the Arts.* Harcourt, Brace & World, Inc., 1968.

The Memorial History of Boston: 1630-1880. 4 vols. Justin Winsor, ed. James R. Osgood and Company, 1881.

Richardson, E. P., *Painting in America: From 1502 to the Present.* Thomas Y. Crowell Company, 1965.

Whitley, William T., *Artists and Their Friends in England, 1700-1799.* 2 vols. Benjamin Blom, London, 1928.

EXHIBITION CATALOGUES AND PERIODICALS

Burroughs, Alan, "Young Copley." *Art in America,* Vol. XXXI (Oct. 1943), pp. 161-171.

Paintings by John Singleton Copley. Metropolitan Museum of Art, 1936-1937.

The World of Benjamin West. Allentown Art Museum, 1962.

Acknowledgments

For their help in the preparation of this book, the author and editors wish to thank the following persons and institutions: Mrs. Robert Barclay, Reading, Massachusetts; Mrs. George Bumgardner, American Antiquarian Society, Worcester, Massachusetts; Mrs. Ropes Cabot, Bostonian Society, Boston; Miss Winifred Collins, Massachusetts Historical Society, Boston; Mrs. H. B. Crooks, Worcester Art Museum, Worcester, Massachusetts; Philip H. Dunbar, Connecticut Historical Society, Hartford; Arthur L. Finney, A.I.D., Royall House Association, Medford, Massachusetts; Mrs. James J. Keeney, Old Sturbridge Village, Sturbridge, Massachusetts; Karen McWhirter, Metropolitan Museum of Art, New York; Mrs. William Nary, Yale University Art Gallery, New Haven; David Pickman, Museum of Fine Arts, Boston; Mrs. Caroline Rollins, Yale University Art Gallery, New Haven; Royall House Association, Medford, Massachusetts; Clifford W. Shaefer, Collection of Edgar and Bernice Chrysler Garbisch, New York; Richard L. Tooke, Museum of Modern Art, New York; Diggery Venn, Museum of Fine Arts, Boston; Mrs. Eliza M. Webster, Fogg Art Museum, Cambridge, Massachusetts; Mrs. Gilian Wohlauer, Museum of Fine Arts, Boston.

Picture Credits

The sources for the illustrations in this book appear below. Credits for pictures from left to right are separated by semicolons, from top to bottom by dashes.

SLIPCASE: Frederick G. S. Clow courtesy Museum of Fine Arts, Boston.

FRONT END PAPERS: Courtesy Museum of Fine Arts, Boston.

BACK END PAPERS: Courtesy Museum of Fine Arts, Boston.

CHAPTER 1: 6—I. N. Phelps Stokes Collection, The New York Public Library. 8 —Eliot Elisofon. 11—American Antiquarian Society. 12—Eliot Elisofon. 13—Edmond De Beaumont courtesy Worcester Art Museum—© National Portrait Gallery, London. 14—The Connecticut Historical Society. 15 —*The Massachusetts Magazine* (March 1789). 19—City Art Museum of St. Louis. 21—Lee Boltin. 22—Yale University Art Gallery; Frederick G. S. Clow—Prints Division, The New York Public Library, Astor, Lenox and Tilden Foundations. 23—Courtesy Museum of Fine Arts, Boston. 24—Lee Boltin; Courtesy Museum of Fine Arts, Boston. 25—William Abbenseth; Lee Boltin. 26, 27—Yale University Art Gallery; Courtesy Harvard University —Courtesy Museum of Fine Arts, Boston. 28,29—Courtesy Henry Francis du Pont Winterthur Museum. 30—Courtesy Museum of Fine Arts, Boston. 31—Courtesy Museum of Fine Arts, Boston; Santa Barbara Museum of Art. 32—Fogg Art Museum courtesy Harvard University. 33—Lee Boltin. 34, 35—Paulus Lesser.

CHAPTER 2: 36—Lee Boltin. 38, 39—American Antiquarian Society. 41—John R. Freeman courtesy British Museum, London. 42—Prints Division, The New York Public Library, Astor, Lenox and Tilden Foundations—The Metropolitan Museum of Art. 47 through 57—Robert Walch.

CHAPTER 3: 58—Courtesy Museum of Fine Arts, Boston. 62—The Toledo Museum of Art, Toledo, Ohio. 64—Courtesy The Henry Francis du Pont Winterthur Museum. 66—P. Hollander Gross. 69—American Antiquarian Society. 71—I. N. Phelps Stokes Collection, The New York Public Library; American Antiquarian Society. 72—Courtesy Museum of Fine Arts, Boston. 73—American Antiquarian Society. 77—Fogg Art Museum courtesy Harvard University. 78—Yale University Art Gallery. 79—The Corcoran Gallery of Art. 80 through 84—Lee Boltin. 85—Fogg Art Museum courtesy Harvard University. 86, 87—Lee Boltin.

CHAPTER 4: 88—Yale University Art Gallery. 90—Fernand Bourges courtesy The Connecticut Historical Society. 92—Courtesy The Wadsworth Atheneum, Hartford, Connecticut. 93—Steve Hansen courtesy Brookline Historical Society. 94, 95—The Metropolitan Museum of Art. 97—Courtesy of the Abby Aldrich Rockefeller Folk Art Collection, Williamsburg, Virginia. 99—Old Sturbridge Village. 100—Worcester Art Museum. 101—Massachusetts Historical Society. 102—Yale University Art Gallery—Ohio State Historical Society. 103—Collection of Edgar William and Bernice Chrysler Garbisch. 104 —Connecticut Historical Society. 105—Collection of Edgar William and Bernice Chrysler Garbisch. 106, 107—The Museum of Modern Art, New York. 108, 109—National Gallery of Art, Washington, D.C. 110, 111—Collection of Edgar William and Bernice Chrysler Garbisch.

CHAPTER 5: 112—National Gallery of Art, Washington, D.C. 115—Both Frank Lerner. Top from *Monumenti Antichi Enediti* by J. J. Winckelmann (1821) —bottom from *Histoire de l'Art chez les Anciens* by J. J. Winckelmann (1802). 116 —The Cleveland Museum of Art. 119—A. J. Wyatt courtesy Philadelphia Museum of Art. 121, 122—Yale University Art Gallery. 123—Courtesy Pennsylvania Academy of the Fine Arts. 124—Courtesy The Brooklyn Museum —Bob Jones University Collection of Sacred Art, Greenville, South Carolina. 125—Lee Boltin. 126, 127—National Gallery of Canada, Ottawa. 128 through 131—National Gallery of Art, Washington, D.C.

CHAPTER 6: 132—Copyright reserved to Her Majesty the Queen. 136—John R. Freeman courtesy British Museum, London. 137—Royal Academy of Arts, London. 138—Alfred Frankenstein from *The Baronetage of England* by the Reverend William Betham (1805). 142—From *John Singleton Copley*, Vol. II, by Jules David Prown, Harvard University Press (1966). 145—Paulus Lesser. 146—Courtesy The Wadsworth Atheneum, Hartford, Connecticut. 147 —Paulus Lesser. 148, 149—National Gallery of Art, Washington, D.C.; Nemo Warr. 150—Lee Boltin. 151 through 155—Derek Bayes. 156-157—Frederick G. S. Clow courtesy Museum of Fine Arts, Boston; Derek Bayes. 158 —Lee Boltin—William B. O'Neil. 159—Courtesy Museum of Fine Arts, Boston.

CHAPTER 7: 160—National Portrait Gallery, London. 162—The Metropolitan Museum of Art. 164—Lent by the Boston Athenaeum courtesy Museum of Fine Arts, Boston. 165—Courtesy Pennsylvania Academy of the Fine Arts. 166—Ralph Thompson courtesy The University of Virginia. 167— Smithsonian Institution. 169—Courtesy Pennsylvania Academy of the Fine Arts. 170, 171—A. J. Wyatt courtesy Philadelphia Museum of Art; Courtesy of The New-York Historical Society, New York City. 172, 173—The Peale Museum, Baltimore. 174—National Gallery of Art, Washington, D.C. 175 —The Cleveland Museum of Art. 176—Barney Burstein courtesy Worcester Art Museum. 177—National Gallery of Art, Washington, D.C. 178, 179 —Collection, Syracuse University. 180 through 183—Yale University Art Gallery.

Index

Numerals in italics indicate a picture of the subject mentioned. Unless otherwise specified, all listed art works are by Copley. Dimensions are given in inches; height precedes width.

189

Index (continued)

The typeface employed in this book is called Janson, after Anton Janson, the Dutch typefounder who popularized it in Leipzig in the late 17th Century. The face was first cut, however, by Nicholas Kis, a Hungarian working in Amsterdam in the 1680s.